Dhikr

The Remembrance of God

AN EXPLANATION BY

M. R. Bawa Muhaiyaddeen

THE FELLOWSHIP PRESS
Philadelphia, Pennsylvania

Library of Congress Cataloging-in-Publication Data

Muhaiyaddeen, M. R. Bawa.
    Dhikr : the remembrance of God / by M. R. Bawa Muhaiyaddeen.
       p.   cm.
    ISBN 0-914390-53-8. — ISBN 0-914390-54-6
    1. God (Islam)—Worship and love. 2. God (Islam)—Name—Prayerbooks and
devotions. 3. Sufism—Doctrines. 4. Prayer—Islam. 5. Islamic hymns.   I. Title.
BP189.62.M6243 1999
297.3'82—dc21   99-17828
                                                               CIP

Printed in the United States of America
by THE FELLOWSHIP PRESS
Bawa Muhaiyaddeen Fellowship
First Printing: Revised and Expanded Edition

Muhammad Raheeem Bawa Muhaiyaddeen ﴾رضه﴿

Table of Contents

Editor's Note ix

Introduction xi

ONE / The Constant Remembrance 3

TWO / With Every Breath 35

THREE / Questions and Answers 57

FOUR / The Prayer of a Sufi 67

FIVE / The Power of the Dhikr 79

SIX / Become One with God 83

Appendix

1. The Twenty-eight Letters within Man:
   Explanation and Illustrations 87

2. The Nine Muhammads 95

3. The Inner Meaning of the Diacritical Marks 99

4. Sūratul-Fātihah and Sūratul-Ikhlās:
   Translation and Commentary 103

5. The Seven Levels of Consciousness 109

Glossary 111

Editor's Note

Dhikr: The Remembrance of God by Muhammad Raheem Bawa Muhaiyaddeen ☺ was first published in 1975. Many readers found that in order to truly understand this unique prayer, further clarification and explanation was necessary. In response to this need, the original Tamil manuscript was re-edited by the original translator, Dr. K. Ganesan, with contributions from Mrs. Rajes Ganesan and Dr. Usha Balamore. To further enrich the original material, several new selections were chosen from the archives of The Bawa Muhaiyaddeen Fellowship. These discourses comprise Chapters Five and Six, as well as the last three questions in Chapter Three.

The reader will note some alterations from the original text. First is the change of spelling from *zikr* to *dhikr*. There is no English equivalent for the Arabic letter *dhāl* (ذ). The closest sound in English is 'th' as pronounced in 'thee' or 'this'. After discussing the many problems of transliteration with Bawa Muhaiyaddeen, the Fellowship Press adopted the present spelling in 1981.

Bawa Muhaiyaddeen also instructed that the order of the first two chapters be reversed. He felt that the explanations and inner meanings of the *dhikr* should precede the specific directions on how to perform this prayer.

In Chapter One, now titled *The Constant Remembrance*, the reader will note several footnotes designated by letters, in addition to the standard numerical footnotes. These are further explanations given at a later date by Bawa Muhaiyaddeen, often in response to a question. In the first edition these were inserted into the text, but in this revised edition, it was decided to place them at the bottom of the page in order to preserve the continuity of the original talk. These explanations given by Bawa Muhaiyaddeen should not be confused with the numerical footnotes, which were provided by translators and editors.

Chapter Six, *Become One with God*, was also given at a later date. Originally added at the end of the aforementioned chapter, it now appears separately.

Numerous Arabic terms appear in italics throughout the text. Although these words are commonly spoken throughout the Islamic world, Bawa Muhaiyaddeen's usage often encompasses deeper mystical meanings. Therefore, extensive definitions of all these terms have been provided in the Glossary. Occasionally, to help the Western reader, either the transliteration or a simplified translation has been inserted in brackets.

Also, to enhance readability, the honorific phrases customarily mentioned after the names of prophets, angels, and saints have been denoted by calligraphic circles. Their meanings can be found in the Glossary. For example, the calligraphic circle (☺) stands for *sallallāhu 'alaihi wa sallam*, peace and blessings be upon him. This is the traditional supplication spoken after the name of Prophet Muhammad, the Final Prophet, the Messenger of God. Frequently in this text, Bawa Muhaiyaddeen is speaking of the essence or light of *Muhammad* that has existed since the primal beginning [*āthi*] and will exist for eternity. Again for clarification, we have italicized the many names for this state, such as *Nūr Muhammad*, *Muhammadiyyah*, *Ahamad*. However, it must be understood that Bawa Muhaiyaddeen never differentiated between these two, the Prophet and the light. For in truth, like the fragrance and the rose, they are inextricably intertwined.

These changes and additions were done with the intention of furthering the reader's understanding of this most exalted prayer. We pray that our limited understanding has in no way infringed upon the beauty and depth of Bawa Muhaiyaddeen's teachings, and we humbly ask forgiveness for any shortcomings or mistakes.

Special thanks should be given to the many members of the Bawa Muhaiyaddeen Fellowship who worked on this project with untiring devotion, every step of the way, from typing, editing, and proofreading to printing, collating, and binding.

May God bless this venture, and may this reservoir of wisdom quench the inner thirst of all who read it.

Introduction

Bismillāhir-Rahmānir-Rahīm. In the name of God, the Most Merciful, Most Compassionate.

God created man as the most exalted being. Endowed with God's radiant light and with seven levels of consciousness, man is the only creation that has the capacity to realize himself and his Creator and to understand the meaning of his own existence. If a man can totally free himself of the attachments and pulls of mind and desire, if he can say with every breath, "Nothing other than God is real. Only God exists," then he will live in a state of bliss. He will be merged with God, and his wisdom will be a source of nourishment for all lives.

Although God created all human beings with the potential to live in this state, ever since the time of the Prophet Adam ☉, people gradually became enmeshed in the pleasures of this physical world and began to worship deities and forces other than God.

Seeing this decline, God sent special beings called prophets to the earth. Filled with the light and wisdom of God, they brought direct revelations of His truths to mankind and showed them how to return to their inherent state of exalted wisdom and oneness with God. Each prophet came with the same message. Moses, Jesus, Muhammad (may the peace of God be upon them), and many others all spoke of the existence of the one God who alone was worthy of worship. After Muhammad ☉, no more prophets were sent with these direct messages.

In addition to the prophets, another type of being was also needed, a being fully imbued with the resonance of God's truth, a divine being. Such beings, known as *qutbs*, were sent to reveal the inner meanings of the revelations brought earlier by the prophets. The power of the *qutb*, called the *qutbiyyat*, is always present in this world. It exists within the vibration and resonance of truth and wisdom in all lives. It is the state of consciousness called divine analytic wisdom, which explains the point within man where the connection to God exists. It resonates within, guiding man's every action. It shows him the right and the wrong in everything, so he can, with faith, certitude, and determination, pursue what is good.

It is rare to find such a being in this world, a true *qutb*. Shaikh Muhammad Raheem Bawa Muhaiyaddeen ☺, the author of this book, is just such a one. Where did he come from and who was he? Only God knows. Bawa Muhaiyaddeen was seen in the mid-1930's in the jungles of Sri Lanka, near the holy mountains of Gīlānī and Kataragama. Two pilgrims from Jaffna came across him sitting under a tree in meditation. Recognizing his special character, they invited him to return with them and be their teacher. He told them to return exactly one year later to the same tree. They did and Bawa Muhaiyaddeen was there. He promised he would appear at their house in Jaffna a few weeks later. On the promised day, the two sat and waited. They had not given him any directions, not even their address. Near dusk, they looked up and saw Bawa Muhaiyaddeen standing in the doorway. This was the beginning of his public life.

In time, more and more people came from all over Sri Lanka to seek advice from this remarkable gnostic. Eventually some of the seekers joined together and formed the Serendib Sufi Study Circle. Those seeking the truth within themselves stayed to study with him. For them, he was like a resonating tuning fork that could set off the same resonance within them, a resonance by which one could monitor his own state. But that was only part of it. Bawa Muhaiyaddeen was so much more than anyone could ever describe.

In the late sixties, Bawa Muhaiyaddeen was invited to the United States. He came in October of 1971, and shortly after that a Fellowship was formed to record and preserve his teachings and to spread the wealth of his wisdom to all those who seek it. Bawa Muhaiyaddeen transcended his mortal form in December 1986 and is buried near Philadelphia, Pennsylvania.

In 1974, several Americans went to Sri Lanka to live at the feet of this holy man. This was all so new to us. I recall a time when we were sitting peacefully on the floor of his second story room. It was a typical steamy tropical day, and wisps of diesel exhaust and kerosene fumes from the kitchens wafted through the heavy air. Tiny arboreal birds called bulbuls were singing with huge voices, magpie robins flitted around, and the ever present crows squawked at each other, keeping a wary watch for any edible morsel. Someone swept a dead mouse off the second floor balcony and a crow swooped down and grabbed it in midair, before it could even hit the ground. We were growing used to such things. We learned to put up with the many mosquitoes and to expect all sorts of tropical adventures. Although these things were colorful, they soon ceased to matter. Our goal was to reach the state of oneness with God. We were there to learn.

One day Bawa Muhaiyaddeen told us to gather at 4:30 p.m. the following day, when he would give us initiation. We wondered about what was going to happen. We had heard of initiation by laying a hand on the head, or by being given a special word or words [*mantras*], but we had never seen Bawa Muhaiyaddeen do any of these. In fact, we had never heard Bawa Muhaiyaddeen talk of initiation before.

So we all gathered, defying a local curfew, and waited with great expectation. But what occurred was both a surprise and delight. He began to talk about the *dhikr*. For some time he had promised to give us an explanation of this meditation. The ultimate and long-awaited moment had come. For us, it was like suddenly having the meaning of life gush forth, after long years of searching for it. It began as a talk about how to recite the *dhikr* and then grew into a series of related talks which tied in every aspect of life. Bawa Muhaiyaddeen talked about God, wisdom, the prophets, religions, how to overcome ignorance—everything. This book includes many of those talks. It shows the secrets of this path and offers a way of life for those who believe in God.

Dhikr means remembrance, the constant remembrance of God. The remembrance that Bawa Muhaiyaddeen gave us was expressed with the Arabic words: "*Lā ilāha:* There is no other deity. *Illallāhu:* Only the one God truly exists." The first part is said with the outgoing breath and the second on the incoming breath. However, the breathing is not the focus, but rather the meaning within the words. I have always felt it wise to not get hung up on words or language. All the prophets spoke some version of a Semitic language, such as Hebrew, Aramaic, or Arabic, depending on where they were from. Bawa Muhaiyaddeen spoke Tamil, the ancient Dravidian language of Southern India and Sri Lanka, but much Arabic was mixed into his speech. He sometimes called God by the name *Āndavan*, which is Tamil. Often he referred to God as Allah. The word Allah in Arabic means God, but that word does not belong to any particular religion. It is simply the name for God spoken by all who live in Arabic speaking lands. A friend who grew up in Jesus' birthplace of Nazareth remembered the local Roman Catholic priest using the name Allah and saying, "*Al-hamdu lillāh:* All praise is to God." God is God, no matter what name He is called by. There is only one God. The remembrance, or *dhikr*, spoken of in this book, is the remembrance of that one God.

To remember is to follow a path, a groove, that has been cut into one's consciousness. Everything we do creates a memory path. The mind can travel along one of those grooves in order to recapture the feelings, energy, and qualities of some original event. Thus, when we indulge in evil actions, we risk cutting a new groove that could later open up to the wandering mind. The point of *dhikr*, then, is to reopen the memory path leading to that exalted state of oneness with God from which we all came. It is the most primordial point of our existence, the place where our soul connects God to our physical existence. It is what makes us human beings. This groove within our consciousness goes to that point where God exists. Within that point is the truth and grace of God, the light and wisdom of the prophets, and the resonance of the *qutbiyyat* which explains. We need to cut that groove to God. That is what this book is about.

Dhikr: The Remembrance of God shows the *dhikr* to be the fundamental principle of prayer and reveals the mystical meaning of its twenty-seven letters—the form of the light of the essence of God. It includes a section on how to do the *dhikr* as well as a description of how the *dhikr* and belief in God lead to the evolution of the five outer and six inner duties of Islam. Bawa Muhaiyaddeen also discusses the explaining nature of the *qutbiyyat* and relates an exalted meaning of two *sūrats*, from the Holy Qur'an.

Three types of *dhikr* are described: *adh-dhikrul-jalī* [recited out loud and connected to the physical realm], *adh-dhikrul-qalbī* [done quietly in the heart], and *adh-dhikrur-rūhī* [done by the soul intermingling and merging with God]. If all of these are functioning, then whenever a question arises from within us, the answer will come immediately and be understood by every fiber of our being.

Dhikr is the prayer of the Sufi. It goes on with every breath. It must be practiced with focus and concentration. It will take us to that Power.

The *dhikr* is like an electric current, necessary to light the bulb of wisdom. Once one's intention is set with faith and certitude, this remembrance will flow automatically. But in order to have it flow correctly, it is necessary to conquer attachments, worldly connections, and the pull of mind and desire. Many have found it helpful to get up in the early morning (around four a.m.) to practice.

In essence, this book intertwines many themes: the revelations of the prophets, the levels of wisdom and consciousness, prayer and meditation, and the truth of Islam, or purity, as a way of life for those who believe in God. It should be read, studied, discussed, and practiced. May we all understand its meaning and live in the state where each and every breath is the *dhikr. Āmīn. Al-hamdu lillāh:* All praise be to God!

Michael Abdul Jabbar Toomey

Dhikr

The Remembrance
of God

CHAPTER ONE

The Constant Remembrance

*P*rayer, which arises out of resolve and zeal, takes many different forms and is done in every conceivable language. The ways in which Allah's creations worship Him are as limitless as the stars in the sky. Earth, fire, water, air, and ether, the angels and archangels, saints, *qutbs*,[1] *jinns*, fairies, and illumined beings, the stars, sun, and moon—all of them worship and glorify God in countless languages. Even satan and his followers pray to God. The hells, the heavens, the celestial maidens [*houri*], human beings [*insān*], beasts, reptiles, birds, illusion [*māyā*], and countless others worship Allah in a multitude of ways. Some of the more exalted ways of performing prayer and worship will be pointed out here.

God, the One known as *Allāhu*, is incomparable, alone, and eternal. He is without beginning or end, without form or subtle form, without shadow, and without any helpmate. He is not bound by any limit. He shines as truth within truth, as wisdom within wisdom, as the heart within the heart, the *qalb* within the *qalb*. He shines as the incomparable, endless One, a limitless power.

In order that this power might be understood and worshiped, God manifested man, the most exalted of all His creations, distilling him until he reached a state of perfect clarity. This being, created in such a manner, is known as Adam ☺. It is said that forty-two children were born to Adam and Eve ☺ (in Tamil, *Paramasivan* and *Pārvathi*) from twenty-one pregnancies. Those children joined together as twenty-one families. Thus mankind is known as the family of Adam [*Ādam zāth*].[2]

To these human beings God has given the wisdom of His essence [*dhāt*] and the body of His manifestation [*sifāt*]. Within that body He placed that which is permissible [*halāl*] and that which is prohibited [*harām*], as well as goodness and the dark evil of the base desires. Having placed them

---

1. *qutbs* (A) A title used for the great holy men of Islam.

2. *zāth:* An Urdu word meaning children. Bawa Muhaiyaddeen ☺ said that Urdu is the language spoken by fairies.

within, He made the goodness into absolute goodness [*khair*], and the evil [*sharr*] into *shirk*.[3] He made the permissible into goodness and the prohibited into evil. He placed many such understandings within the human body.

The qualities of earth, fire, water, air, and ether, and all that arose from them, as well as what came forth from the grace of His essence, or *dhāt*, were then explained individually. These six were created as the six kinds of lives.[4] Of these, the creation which is mankind, or *insān*, was formed by Allah out of His essence as the life of goodness, the life endowed with wisdom, the wisdom of the *Nūr*.[5] Only this creation, the one that has wisdom, can be called *insān*. This is the sixth kind of life.

But later, those created in the form of man, those children of Adam ☾ who began as one race, split up into different groups, into Hinduism [*Zabūr*], Zoroastrianism [*Jabrāt*], Christianity [*Injīl*], and Islam [*Furqān*]. Having separated themselves into these four sections and into seventy-three groups, they began to glorify God in different ways and different languages. Thus they separated into different forms of worship and different religions. They treat things such as idols, statues, or pictures as equal to God, replacing the worship of God with idol worship, or with the worship of shadows, the worship of base desires [*nafs*], the worship of illusory things [*māyā*], the worship of this world, of created things, of fire, spirits, and eighty-four kinds of air, of the sun, moon, and stars, and of beasts, birds, and reptiles. They look upon these things as gods and pray to them and worship them. Such actions are prevalent.

Divisions arose out of this practice of different kinds of prayer and worship, resulting in the creation of four hundred trillion, ten thousand gods and the separation into various groups of people who worshiped them. This is how the one family of mankind began to separate, and in the process they began to treat God as a god of separations. It is the very creations given the exalted wisdom of man who have done this! All this happened because man did not understand the divine analytic wisdom

---

3. *shirk* (A) The most serious of all sins, to hold anything as equal to or in association with God.

4. six kinds of lives: The lives of the five elements (earth, fire, water, air, and ether), and the human life, which originates directly from the essence of God.

5. *Nūr* (A) The light of God, the seventh of the seven levels of wisdom innate in man; divine luminous wisdom, the wisdom that enables man to see that he exists within God, and that God exists within him. It is the resplendent wisdom innate in man and which can be awakened. God is the wisdom within that wisdom.

within him, or his soul, that life which is the *dhāt*, the essence of God.

God, therefore, sent the prophets and *qutbs* as His representatives to explain about prayer and to instill in the people the absolute certitude, free of the slightest doubt, that God is One and that there is none worthy of worship other than the one God, *Allāhu ta'ālā*.[6] These prophets and *qutbs* were sent to firmly establish prayer, to enlighten the people's wisdom, and to strengthen their *īmān* [absolute certitude of faith] in the one God.

One hundred and twenty-four thousand representatives came to prove the existence of God. They came to give certitude to wisdom, *īmān*, and faith. However, in accordance with whatever state people were in, they accepted and followed the different prophets, and, holding fast to their belief in a particular prophet, created separate religions based upon their beliefs. This resulted in divisions among mankind. The prophets all came as representatives of the one God, to teach the children of Adam ﷺ about God and to make them accept Him, but instead they accepted His prophets and followed them. And, since there were many prophets, the people, by following them, have created many religions.

One hundred and twenty-four thousand representatives of God have appeared. This is the decreed limit, and that limit has been reached. However, despite the message they all brought about the one power that has no equal or parallel and is beyond limit, the people still did not understand. Each group ascribed to that limitless power a beginning and an end. They also set a limit on when prayers should begin and end. And so there exists a prescribed limit for prayers done in any language.

Thus, instead of following the One who is limitless, the people began to follow their particular prophet and to worship in a limited manner, praying to forms or formless things, to spirits, to base desires and cravings, or to the mind. The people, with their happinesses and sorrows and a million different thoughts and intentions, placed their own states in front of themselves and prayed to them with a prayer which has a time limit. Such prayers take only two to five minutes to finish. It is people that have created these limits, these beginnings and ends. These are the ways that have prevailed in the world from the time Adam ﷺ was created until today.

---

6. *Allāhu ta'ālā* (A) *Allāhu:* The beautiful, undiminishing One. *Ta'ālā:* the One who exists in all lives in a state of humility and exaltedness. Lit. God, the most high.

In every man, this state exists as the opium called religion and dogma. One who imbibes this opium cannot look up with discernment. Lacking the discrimination of divine analytic wisdom, he bends his head down and gazes at the place of birth, the section of creation. Instead of using his divine analytic wisdom to discriminate and look up at God's *dhāt*, the essence which is His grace, he succumbs to the intoxication of this opium that makes his head droop and droop and droop. His neck and his heart bend and bend until his head droops down to look at the place of birth, of creation, the place from which he urinates. Thus his ability to see discriminatively disappears, and so does the wisdom and intelligence to realize, the wisdom to understand, the divine analytic wisdom to separate right from wrong, and the divine luminous wisdom to understand clearly and extract what needs to be extracted. Due to this opium, his feeling, awareness, intellect, assessment, subtle wisdom, divine analytic wisdom, and divine luminous wisdom—all seven levels of consciousness—become drugged.

When he is in this state, intoxicated and bent over, looking down at the place of birth, he is looking toward the very place where religious fanaticism originates. If at that time he suddenly hears, "Wake up! Wake up! Why are you in this drugged state? Why do you keep looking there?" he will immediately start resisting. If a *shaikh* who is an *insān kāmil*,[7] a representative of God, taps him with wisdom and awakens him, saying, "Wake up! Wake up! Why are you looking there?" he will retort, "Who are you? Go away!" and proclaim, "My religion! Your religion!" and begin to fight. He will start wars, commit murders, and perform human sacrifices and other evil acts. These are the battlefields of those intoxicated by the opium of religions. When awakened, such a one will immediately start fighting and even be willing to commit murder. Due to the intoxication from the opium, he will be lacking the wisdom that discriminates, and so will not know good from evil. Therefore his every action will be a battle. Without any fear or compassion, without even so much as a thought, he will commit many atrocities.

There is one thing that we who are children of Adam ☮ must be aware of in our lives. We have to understand the six kinds of lives. We have to understand the separations and differences that exist among the

---

7. *insān kāmil* (A) A perfected, God-realized human being; one who has realized Allah as his only wealth, cutting away all the wealth of the world.

children of Adam ⌣ and understand how much evil results from the arrogance associated with the opium of religion.

In order to dispel such darkness and ignorance and to reveal the wisdom of His essence, God gathered together the teachings He had given to the 124,000 prophets who were His representatives, informing them of:

> His glory, His qualities and actions,
> His patience, tolerance, peacefulness, and justice,
> the story of His eternal state,
> the explanations concerning His creations,
> His quality of protectiveness and of sustaining all lives by giving
>   them food,
> His quality of summoning back all the lives He created,
>   inquiring into their good and bad and giving to each of them
>   their appropriate station,
> the Day of Judgment,
>   and the conditions governing the beginning and end of
>   creation.

[He also gathered together the stories regarding the prophets]

> the teachings and commandments He had given to them,
>   their qualities,
> the difficulties they experienced in the world and the
>   hardships they faced:
>   the worship that is done by the people using idols
>   in place of God,
>   the magics and *mantras* used to invoke the
>   elements, and the qualities that worship these
>   elements as gods.

Ultimately, having gathered together all of these and countless other explanations, taking all the commandments He had taught the prophets, all the verses and the chapters, taking the whole story, the wrong and right, and, manifesting Muhammad ⌣ as the final Prophet,**❶** to this He

---

Footnotes **❶**, **❷**, **❸**, and **❹** are further explanations by Bawa Muhaiyaddeen, given at a later time, often in response to a question.

❶ Allah manifested everything through His light, the *Nūr*. It was that same light which

gave the name *Īmān-Islām*, while to the commandments He gave the names *Thiru Marai, Thiru Qur'ān*, and *Satthiya Vētham.* ❽

With God's treasure, His grace, and His *dhāt*, or essence, and using the true wisdom, the wisdom of that essence, His beauty which is

---

He placed on the forehead of Adam (☼). And from that light He also created the prophets. It was that same light that He made into the inner heart [*aham*], giving it the name *Ahamad*. With that very light He brought forth the beauty of His essence as the beauty of the countenance [*muham*], and gave that the name *Muhammad*.

In all, Allah gave nine different names to that light of the *Nūr*.

It is with that light that Allah manifested the form of *Anāthi Muhammad. Anāthi* [the beginningless beginning] is the state before *āthi* [the primal beginning]. It is the state of darkness in which Allah was as Himself, when nothing had been manifested, and only Allah and the *Nūr* existed. In that state, the *Nūr* was given the name *Anāthi Muhammad.* Then Allah brought forth that light of *Nūr* from within Himself, and that was the first, or *Primal Muhammad*, called *Āthi Muhammad.* From that light, from that completeness, Allah manifested the beginning of creation, the world of form, called *awwal*. He brought forth earth, sky, oceans, land, mountains, creations, things that move and things that do not move—everything—from that light, and He gave it the name *Awwal Muhammad.* When He fed those lives with the food that came from that light in the form of atoms of His grace, He gave that light the name *Anna Muhammad.* Then when the lives were nourished by that food and grew from imbibing it, He gave that light the name *Hayāt Muhammad.* In order to fill those lives with that light and make it complete within them, He made that light into the inner heart, or *qalb*, called *aham*, and gave it the name *Ahamad.* When the light of the beauty of that *qalb*, the completeness of *Nūr*, resplended as the beauty of Allah's countenance, He gave that the name *Muhammad.* *Muhammad* combines the beauty of the face [*muham*] and the heart [*aham*]. When the light which was plenitude became complete and effulgent, He saw the completeness and gave it the name *Nūr Muhammad.*

Finally, when that undiminishing resplendent *Nūr* realized its plenitude in Allah, from whom it originally had emerged, Allah gave it the name *Allāh Muhammad.* Having manifested all of creation, that light then lost itself again into that from which it had emerged. Thus the two became one, and Allah gave this the name *Allāh Muhammad.* Allah was *Muhammad* and *Muhammad* was Allah. The two were one. It emerged from that and then lost itself in that and became complete and was given the name *Allāh Muhammad.*

In this way Allah unfolded His light, the *Nūr*, into the nine *Muhammads.* Having brought forth everything from that light, He made it all complete, and then made it all disappear into the completeness. That treasure is what is called *Muhammad.*

Question: Which of these is the *sūrat* of Muhammad (☼)?

Bawa Muhaiyaddeen: The *sūrat* of Muhammad (☼) is the *awwal* form. *Awwal* is the time of manifestation in form. When mankind, or *insān*, was manifested, that is when Muhammad (☼) appears as a form. See Appendix: *The Nine Muhammads*, p. 95.

❽ The name *Satthiya Vētham* means that these commandments originated from God's truth and God's justice, as testimony that they came directly from Him, as sounds in the form of revelations. But in order for the people to realize this, Gabriel (☼) was sent as a heavenly

Muhammad accepted His word—this *Thiru Marai*, this *Thiru Qur'ān*,[8] this revelation, its resonances and meanings, and the radiances that shimmered within it. In this way God's beauty, the beauty of His face [*muham*] and the light that is the beauty of His heart [*aham*], received His word and accepted and absorbed it.

Ahamad, Muhammad.[9] In the *Thiru Qur'ān*, *Ahamad* is the *aham*, the perfectly pure heart, and *Muhammad* is the beauty of Allah's countenance. It confirms that it was these two—*Ahamad* (the *qalb* which is His light) and *Muhammad* (the beauty of His countenance)—that accepted His sounds, the 6,666 vibrations. The proof of this truth, along with the story told to the earlier prophets and the story that later descended in the form of verses to *Muhammad*—all of these were given the name *Thiru Qur'ān.* ◉

---

8. *Thiru Qur'ān* or *Thiru Marai* (T) The primal scripture; the inner *Qur'ān* inscribed within the heart of man. In Tamil *marai* means sacred writing and *thiru* means divine. Bawa Muhaiyaddeen frequently uses the word *thiru* as a prefix to mean three or triple, as in *Thiruchudar*, the Triple Flame.

9. *Ahamad (Ahmad)* (A) Lit. the most praiseworthy; a name frequently given to the Prophet Muhammad ☙. Bawa Muhaiyaddeen says *Ahamad* in order to stress the connection with the Tamil word *'aham'* meaning 'inner heart'. Then, together with *muham*, the Tamil word for countenance, *Muhammad* becomes the light of the inner heart and the beauty of Allah's countenance.

---

messenger to convey those sounds. Those revelations came as grace from God's grace, and upon reaching us, became a vibration.

Question: Does it come as a vibration?

Bawa Muhaiyaddeen: It is a light, God's light. It is His resplendence, His grace that He gives.

Question: So it is not the word of Allah? It is His grace?

Bawa Muhaiyaddeen: The grace is His word! Once it goes forth from Him, it resplends as words. If it were not in word form, people would not understand it. That grace came to Gabriel ☙ and was conveyed to Muhammad ☙, as a revelation, or *wahy*. Only after it had been received by Muhammad ☙ was it called a revelation.

After it is received by man and comes forth from man, it becomes a vibration. Vibration implies movement. Grace has no movement. It comes automatically.

Question: Why was it necessary for Gabriel ☙ to bring the revelations? Cannot Allah speak to Muhammad ☙ directly?

Bawa Muhaiyaddeen: Direct communion did occur. The name *hadīth qudsī* was given to the limitless communication which took place directly between Allah and Muhammad ☙, without the medium of Gabriel ☙. But many people did not accept that they came from God. So when the 6,666 verses came down as commandments, it was necessary to have a witness. This is why Gabriel ☙ brought them. He came as a witness, to establish the proof that Muhammad ☙ was the true Messenger of Allah. For instance, if you and I spoke to each other directly without any witness, who would accept that we spoke?

◉ **Question:** Is this what is meant by *lailatul-qadr*?

Bawa Muhaiyaddeen: We are the *lailatul-qadr*. This is our form, or *sūrat*. The day that the

In accordance with that name, the sound of Allah's essence, His *dhāt*, which is *Īmān-Islām*, resonates as the meaning within the *Thiru Qur'ān*. The resonance and the meaning are both within the *Thiru Qur'ān*. The sound of that essence is *Īmān-Islām*. The sounds of the clear meanings that resonate from it form *Īmān-Islām*. That is what *Īmān-Islām* is.

Allah rolled up and gathered together those sounds (the 6,666 verses) to fashion the form of the *īmān-kalimah*,[10] which is the form of man. This form of the *kalimah* is an inner form made up of twenty-seven letters.[11] The twenty-seven letters are the light form, or *sūrat*, that speaks to God. That is what the *kalimah* is. This *kalimah*, which is composed of twenty-seven letters, is the form for the light called *Ahamad* and *Muhammad*.

What is called *Īmān-Islām* is the resonances and explanations heard when the form of the *kalimah* listens to and speaks with God. *Īmān-Islām* is the perfectly pure *Qur'ān*, the *Thiru Qur'ān*. It is made up of twenty-eight letters. This is God's grace, the grace of God's essence, the treasure for all three worlds (the beginning, this world, and the hereafter). This is the ultimate story. The 6,666 verses, the prophets and their stories, their sorrows and joys, their gains and losses are all compressed and contained within the twenty-eight letters which compose *Īmān-Islām*.

It was to the light of God's essence known as *Ahamad* and to His beauty known as *Muhammad*, to this form which is both the beauty and the light

---

10. *īmān-kalimah* (A) The affirmation of absolute faith in the one God: *Lā ilāha illallāh; Muhammadur-Rasūlullāh*. There is nothing other than You, O God. Only You are Allah, and Muhammad is the Messenger of Allah.

11. The twenty-seven letters: Of the twenty-eight letters of the Arabic alphabet, which constitute the subtle body of man, twenty-seven comprise the *sūrat*, or form, of the *Īmān-kalimah*. All twenty-eight letters together are the form of *Īmān-Islām*. The *Thiru Qur'ān* and the *Thiru Marai*, including the 6,666 verses, are compressed within these twenty-eight letters. See Appendix: *The Twenty-eight Letters within Man: Explanation and Illustrations*, p. 87.

---

kathir, or ray of the soul, descends from the world of souls into the body is called lailatul-qadr. Thus that is our form. And when the soul communes with Allah, that is the day of mi'rāj. Of the twenty-seven letters which form the kalimah, the first letter to come is the lailatul-qadr, while the twenty-seventh letter is the mi'rāj, the communion with Allah. Both occur at the same time. The kalimah, which is our form, begins in the lailatul-qadr and ends in the mi'rāj. Thus when the form of the kalimah comes into being, the ray of the soul descends, and when imān is perfect, communion takes place. Communion with Allah is possible only when imān develops. How can one communicate with God if he has not realized the twenty-seven letters? Once he knows these letters, he has no existence; 'he' has died, and on that day meets and communes with Allah. The Nūr communes with Allah.

of His essence, that the *Thiru Qur'ān,* the *Thiru Marai,* and *Īmān-Islām,* the sounds of communion with Him, were sent down. To commune with God through the twenty-seven letters is *mi'rāj.*[12] *Mi'rāj* means to converse with Allah in the place where He dwells. That is where *Muhammad-Ahamad* communes with the king of kings, in the station of the *'arsh* [throne of God, crown of the head], where the king of kings dwells. This is the state of *mi'rāj.* **❶**

Speaking with the king of kings is what is known as *mi'rāj.* This is the station of *Muhammad-Ahamad,* the light, speaking to the resplendence known as *Īmān-Islām* or the *Thiru Qur'ān.* All of the 6,666 verses—all of

---

12. *mi'rāj* (A) The night journey of the Prophet Muhammad ⊕ through the heavens to commune with Allah. Here Bawa Muhaiyaddeen is referring to the beauty of Allah's light in the heart [*Ahamad*] and Allah's beauty in the face [*Muhammad*] of a perfectly pure human being meeting and conversing with Allah.

---

❶ The *Thiru Marai* is the secret of the three realms—the universe of the soul, of this world, and of the next world.

The *Thiru Qur'ān* is the Triple Flame: *Allāh, Muhammad,* and *Muhaiyaddeen. Allāh,* His essence which is *Muhammad,* and the *Qutbiyyat,* or *Muhaiyaddeen,* which is the wisdom that explains the truth of God—these three effulgences reveal the meaning of the plenitude that has been given the name *Thiru Qur'ān.* The perfectly pure effulgence of *Allāh,* His essence which is His grace [*Ahamad* and *Muhammad*], and the *Qutbiyyat* which has Allah's *wilāyāt,* the powers with which He performs His duties—these three are given forth as light, as the Triple Flame. The *Thiru Qur'ān* is the word of the grace of these three resplendences and the power of that word. This power of Allah exists both inside and outside of all His creations.

Ahamad and *Muhammad* are Allah's quality of goodness, which is His essence, His *dhāt.* His essence fills all lives and has compassion for all lives. It protects everything.

The *Qutbiyyat* exists in all lives as the revelations, the vibrations, the powers, and the clarity of wisdom, which is divine analytic wisdom, or the sixth level of consciousness. It explains the meanings within wisdom. It sees what is right and wrong and shows it to man [*insān*]. It sees Allah and it explains the meaning of the ninety-nine divine names [*asmā'ul-husnā*] which constitute Allah's *sūrat,* or form. It shows the path of the ninety-nine attributes within that form and the qualities and *wilāyāt* with which Allah performs His duties. The ultimate name, the one-hundredth name, which is Allah, comes as a resonance. It is His plenitude of perfect purity, the plenitude within the plenitude. The *Qutbiyyat,* resonating and shining, explains and reveals all of this. It is a light, a vibration, called *Qutbhū.* It exists as His grace within grace, as divine wisdom.

Joined together as purity, these three—*Allāh,* His essence (*Ahamad* and *Muhammad*), and *Qutbiyyat*—these three graces, these three powers, these teachings and their meanings, form the treasure which is called the *Thiru Qur'ān.* The explanation is given by the *guru* to man in three facets. *Thiru Guru-Ān.* This is the *guru* or *shaikh* to wisdom, to grace, and to life, or *hayāt*—to perfect purity (*Nūr*), to the *dhāt* (*Muhammad*), and to the *wilāyāt* (*Qutbiyyat*). Thus everything—is contained within these twenty-eight letters. If one understands this, he understands the ocean of divine knowledge, the *bahrul-'ilm.* Only if one understands *Ahamad* can one understand the *kalimah.* Only if one understands *Muhammad* can one understand the limitless beauty of Allah. Only if one understands *Īmān-Islām* can one understand

---

it exists as the *guru* in three ways. All this is given the name *Thiru Qur'ān.* The three meanings resonating as one constitute the *Thiru Qur'ān.*

This is but a small explanation, an abbreviated meaning of the *Thiru Qur'ān.* There are millions of meanings. The world calls this *Allāh, Muhammad,* and *Muhaiyaddeen* (the *Qutb*). If the real meaning were to be told in its full power and glory, the extent of it could never be unfolded. It has no end. We have to understand and realize what the *Thiru Qur'ān* is. Think about it. This is the *guru,* or *shaikh,* to the universe of the soul, to the universe of Allah's essence or grace, and to the perfectly pure universe of your life, which exists forever as the grace, the *rahmat,* of the *rahmatul-'ālamīn.* Thus the *Thiru Qur'ān* exists as the *guru* in all three universes, the universe of the soul, the universe of Allah's essence [*dhāt*], and the universe of His throne [*dhāhuth*], the universe in which He is king. It exists as the *shaikh* to life.

∞

Question: You spoke of *Thiru Guru-Ān.* You say that God is the only male. But God is said to be neither male nor female. [*Thiru* means triple or three; *guru* is the equivalent for *shaikh;* and *Ān* means male. Allah is the only male. All creation have desire and are female, longing for the One who is male. Thus *Thiru Guru-Ān* is Allah, who is the *guru,* or *shaikh,* to man in the three realms].

Bawa Muhaiyaddeen: He is resplendence. When you see Him, He can be seen only as a resplendence. That, like the letter *alif* (I) by itself has no sound. The mouth is open, as though to say 'A-a-a', but no sound comes forth. Only when a *fathah* (Í) is placed above the *alif* does the sound come, "Aaah!". Only when man becomes the *fathah* and joins with the *alif* does the sound come forth saying, "Allah." If the mark [*kasrah*] falls below the *alif* (I), the sound is "Eeee." That indicates the *dunyā,* the world. If the *dhammah* is placed above the *alif* (Í), the sound is "Oooo," which is calling to Him, saying, *"Allāhū."* His resonance has come. Sound has come. Speech has come. The *dhāt,* the essence, has come. Only then does man speak with Allah. That is the *dhāt.*

Only after the three have been placed—*fathah* above the *alif* (Í), *kasrah* below the *alif* (I), and *dhammah* above the *alif* (Í), does it become *Allāhū.* Now man will be able to speak as the essence [*dhāt*]. Only then is there sound, vibration. Only then does speech begin. The *dhāt* has come.

Alif by itself has no sound. Man must bring Allah to life within. He must become the *fathah.* Right now he is below, in the *kasrah.* He is buried in the mud. He must move up.

Once you move up, the sound begins, and you and He can speak. That is, *Nūr Muhammad* is speaking to Allah. Now the revelations [*wahys*] will come. Now you have to speak. You will not speak with this tongue, but with the resplendent tongue of *īmān.* See Appendix: *The Twenty-eight Letters within Man: Explanation and Illustrations* and *The Inner Meaning of the Seven Diacritical Marks,* pp. 87 and 99.

the *Qur'ān*. One who does not understand this is called satan, the *kāfir*, or unbeliever, who talks behind one's back.

That which will explain and elucidate this story is the light-form called *Ahamad* and Allah's beauty known as *Muhammad*. This is the secret inner form [*sūratul-hikmat*], the Messenger that came as the helper for *awwal*, *dunyā*, and *ākhirah* [the beginning, this world, and the hereafter], the inner form of Allah's essence that is *Ahamad* and *Muhammad*. The story of that secret form is Allah's story. If one understands the story of the *Thiru Marai*, the story of *Īmān-Islām*, and the story of the *kalimah*, he will understand that that is the *Qur'ān*, the ocean of divine knowledge. Even if all the water in the world were made into ink, and all the wood in the world were made into pens and they were used to write about the form [*sūrat*] of this *kalimah* and the *Thiru Qur'ān* known as *Īmān-Islām*, the explanation could never be completed. Even if we tried repeatedly, we could never encompass it all. It is limitless. We have to understand this.

All living creations were given an explanation of this *Thiru Marai*, so they might pray with understanding. The light called *Ahamad* and *Muhammad* provided explanations to the six kinds of lives—trees, plants, vines, grasses, shrubs, birds, human beings, beasts, *jinns*, fairies, angels, and all living creations—at the correct time for each and befitting their level of wisdom. Milk was given to the one who needs milk. Rice was given to the one who eats rice. Fruit was given to the one who eats fruit. Water was given to one who drinks water. Flesh was given to one who eats flesh. To each was given whatever was needed, appropriate to their level of wisdom.

In this way, *Muhammad*—the form of the *kalimah*, the light of God's essence—gave to the many millions of God's creations the explanations of prayer, the explanations of what is permissible and prohibited, and the meaning of good and evil, in keeping with each one's ability to understand. Different ways of worship appropriate for each were also shown. The prayer, or *vanakkam*, appropriate for an *insān kāmil* was shown to *insān kāmil*. The prayer appropriate for angels was shown to the angels. The prayer appropriate for *jinns* was shown to the *jinns*. The prayer befitting the understanding of the prophets was explained to the prophets. The prayer appropriate for animals was taught to them. In the same way, that which was appropriate for monkeys was taught to the monkeys.

Thus, whatever was suitable for each type of wisdom was explained to each creation in the manner befitting that creation. To those with divine analytic wisdom, explanations were given that would help them understand with discernment. Each one was shown the section of the limitless ocean in which they could bathe. Those who wanted to swim in the ocean were shown the ocean. Those who wanted to swim close to shore were shown the shore. Those who were content to scoop up just a handful of water and bathe with that were shown that. In this manner, with the directive, "You must understand," the grace of Allah and the ways of worship and prayer were shown to each in keeping with their level of wisdom. Thus there exist these different ways, different types, different states, and different steps.

As just a part of the total story, *Īmān-Islām* is usually presented as the five and six duties. In describing it, people commonly say, "The five and six duties must be realized and understood." This is how Islam is understood in the world. However, this is but one part of a vast story.

Thus far, we have been talking about the *Qur'ān.* After we finish speaking about all this, we will connect it to the explanations of prayer and *dhikr.*[13] They are connected, not different from one another. They are the truth of Islam.

All this is the essence of what has been told to the wisdom called *Īmān-Islām.* What we have said so far is but a fraction of the total meaning. It is actually a great matter, for if you come to understand it, you will be able to understand the power of Allah, the power of His essence, His *dhāt.* Understanding this through the seven levels of consciousness [feeling, awareness, intellect, assessment, wisdom, divine analytic wisdom, and divine luminous wisdom] will open up the vast ocean of Allah's grace. However, when understood and explained only by the intellect, these duties seem to be very ordinary. Such explanations, limited to the level of intellect, can be understood easily.

There are five and six obligatory duties, or *furūd,* in *Īmān-Islām.* Of the five, which are outer duties, the first is to accept Allah. The second is

---

13. *dhikr (zikr)* (A) The remembrance of God; in this text it refers to the exalted prayer *lā ilāha, illallāhu* [There is no god but God]. The first letter of the Arabic word *dhikr* is pronounced like the 'th' in 'thee' and 'this'. In the first edition of this book this same word was transliterated as *zikr,* a spelling common in dialects originating in the Levant East. See Editor's Note and Glossary.

to worship Him. The third is charity, or *sadaqah*. The fourth is to observe the fast. The fifth is to go on holy pilgrimage, or *hajj*. These are the five required duties for man to perform. They are very easy to do. But this is a simplified meaning of Islam.

There are also five *waqts*, or times of prayer, which begin at a particular time and end at a particular time. They have a beginning and an end. How many prostrations [*sajdahs*] are done in these prayers? In some, you bow [*rukū'*] seventeen or nineteen times. On Fridays, there is a sermon, or *khutbah*. There is also a specific prayer called *janāzah*, which is recited at a funeral.

Thus, each time of worship and remembrance [*dhikr*] includes several kinds of prayers, prayers said during prostration and prayers said during the fast. But these all have a limited time, a beginning and an end. To practice in this way is called *sharī'at*;[14] it is a required duty, or *fard*. This is an easy way to pray, somewhat like babies at play. This form of prayer suits us when we are still young, just as playing with dolls suits a baby's level of wisdom. It is something we can understand, because it relates to intellect and is the form most acceptable to that level of understanding. This is but one aspect of *īmān* [faith].

For other levels of wisdom, there are different ways of prostrating and worshiping Allah. When an *insān kāmil*, using the strength of his *īmān* and his divine analytic wisdom which separates and discriminates, sets out to contemplate evil and goodness, essence and creation, absolute certitude of faith and surrender to Allah, permissible and prohibited, mankind and beast,[15] good and bad, truth and falsehood, prayer and the explanations relating to prayer; when he reflects on the worship of the one God, the Emperor, the One who accepts prayers, the One worthy of worship, as opposed to the practice of worshiping things other than God as equal to Him; when, analyzing with the discernment of divine analytic wisdom, this *insān kāmil* reflects on the One without limit, the endless, incomparable One, he will realize that all of everything belongs to God—

---

14. *sharī'at* (A) The realization of good and evil and the conducting of one's life according to good. Lit. the first of four steps of spiritual ascendence.

15. *sharr* and *khair*: evil and goodness.
 dhāt and *sifat*: essence and creation.
 īmān and *Islām*: absolute certitude of faith and surrender to Allah.
 halāl and *harām*: permissible and prohibited.
 insān and *hayawān*: mankind and beast.

earth and sky, form, soul, man—everything. Once he realizes with his divine analytic wisdom that everything belongs to his Lord, he will say, "Everything is His. There is nothing that is mine. Heaven is His, this world is His, the body and soul are His. Nothing is mine." When he analyzes, discerns, and understands, he will see only the form and light of the *kalimah*, the form of *insān*. What will the form of this light be? It will resplend as *Ahamad* and *Muhammad*—the *qalb* which is *Ahamad* and the beauty of Allah that is *Muhammad*, both of which are the form of His essence [*dhāt*], the form of grace. An *insān kāmil* will see only this grace.

In that state, he will ask himself, "Who am I?" and with that understanding he will surrender unconditionally and become a slave to God, saying, "I do not exist, *Yā Rahmān*, O Merciful One." When he understands such *īmān* and the form of *Īmān-Islām* within that *īmān*, and when he understands the *kalimah*, he will see nothing but God. He will see no end or beginning to Him. He will see no idols. Once he understands this, everything will be God, and he will accept God unconditionally, knowing there is no god but God and none worthy of worship but God. He will establish faith, determination, and certitude in the belief that there is no other God, and with certainty will surrender his *īmān* to the God who created him. His only treasure will be Allah. He will think, "What do I own? I have nothing. God is my only treasure. He is the only treasure that exists forever." Accepting this, he will begin to place his intention on God and to glorify and worship Him and pray to Him. He will begin to do *dhikr* to God.

In this way, an *insān kāmil* makes himself die by destroying the 'I', by destroying that which says 'I' and 'you'. He puts to death the mind which is the world, and the cravings which are the base desires of illusion. When this happens, his soul, which is his life, will glorify God unceasingly, performing 43,242 prostrations to Him every day, without beginning or end, just as the sun and moon endlessly go around and around.

The light which is the soul, the effulgence which is the *Nūr*, the *kalimah* which is *Ahamad*, and the beauty of His countenance which is *Muhammad* —all of which are Allah's essence—uniting as one, day and night, with no limit, will all glorify Allah continuously. During this glorification, every prostration will be in surrender to the only One worthy of worship. One who does this *dhikr* is an *insān kāmil*, a perfected man.

Having acquired the beauty of the *kalimah* of God's essence (the beauty of God's essence which is *Ahamad* and the light of the countenance of God which is *Muhammad)*, this *insān kāmil* stands in the universe of the soul, the universe of light, and glorifies and remembers the One who resplends in the world of grace as the Grace for all the universes, the *Rahmatul-'ālamīn*, the undiminishing wealth of grace. Such is the worship performed by an *insān kāmil* of *Īmān-Islām*.

The worship done by this *insān kāmil* who is *Ahamad* and *Muhammad* will shine with the resonance and the resplendence of *Nūr Muhammadiyyah*. For him there is no beginning or end to time, no time at all, no fasting, no charity, no *hajj*. These things are not for him, nor are they within him or within his *īmān*. His only possession is Allah. This is the worship which carries the *daulat*, the wealth, of the *kalimah* which is the form of the true *īmān* of an *insān kāmil*. May Allah bestow this grace upon everyone. *Āmīn*.

On the path of Allah's essence, His *dhāt*, this form of prayer belongs rightfully to only one group of people, the true followers of *Ahamad* and *Muhammad*. The other seventy-two groups are divided by their many different kinds of prayer, prayers with time limits, and by discriminations such as *my* house *your* house, *my* possession *your* possession, *my* race *your* race, *my* scripture *your* scripture, and *my* child *your* child. These limitations are created by our bondage and attachments, our intentions and focus. They come from the level of intellect and arise from our mind and desire.

Just as hunger, disease, aging, and death have their respective times, prayers have also been assigned certain times to begin and end. In keeping with this, five obligatory duties and five prescribed times, or *waqts*, of prayer have been decreed. The ways in which these prayers are to be conducted have also been established.

First there is *awwal fajr*, the pre-dawn prayer, and the *subh* or early morning prayer. *Subh* means the time of emergence. Then comes the *zuhr* or noon prayer, and then the *'asr* or afternoon prayer. Next there is the *maghrib* or sunset prayer, which relates to the time of aging or darkening, and finally there is the *'ishā'* or late night prayer, which represents the time of death.

The true meaning of these five times is as follows:

At the time of *subh* prayer, man needs to understand the earth from which he was created and then make his connection to that earth die.

Man's birth, his emergence, is *subh*. If one thinks with wisdom about his connection to earth, along with its four hundred trillion, ten thousand glitters of *māyā*, he will realize that his form, which is connected to Adam (☙), must be made to die. The place from which one was born must be made to die. Once you do this, you will have completed this one *waqt*.

The second time of prayer, *zuhr*, is at noontime, representing the time of man's youth. During this period there are many desires which make him play around and say, "I want this, I want that." At this time of youth, he has many desires and cravings. At this second *waqt*, the mind, the desires, and the connection to this world should be made to die.

The third time of prayer is *'asr*, in the afternoon. This represents the connections of the mind, the blood ties, attachments, differences of race, religion, and scriptures, and the monkey mind, which imitates everything it sees. At this *waqt* man must put to death the cravings that arise between thirty and forty from the connections to his monkey mind and its pranks.

The fourth time of prayer is *maghrib*. This represents man's old age, when his nerves and bones become tired and the period of darkness approaches, when time passes him by and the world chases him off. At this time, when his relatives, his children, and the world push him away, he must free himself from the cravings and desires and the 'make-up' of *māyā*. This make-up, which is the illusory blood ties and attachments that celebrate the body, must be put to death before dusk. The titles and positions of the world, and the beautifying of the body must be put to death. This is the *waqt* of *maghrib*.

The fifth time of prayer is *'ishā'*, at night. *Lā ilāha illallāhu wa innī 'Īsā Rūhullāh*: There is nothing other than You O God. You alone are Allah. Jesus *('Īsā)* is the soul of Allah, and there will be another prophet. At this fifth *waqt* of *'ishā'*, man must understand who he is. He must understand the universe of the soul. He needs to understand his soul, which resplends continuously regardless of the rotation of day and night, and do the *dhikr*, *tasbīh*, and *'ibādat*[16] of the soul. This is the fifth *waqt*, in which the soul sees the Soul within the soul, the One to whom his soul belongs, and worships, performs *'ibādat*, to that One.

These are the meanings of the five *waqts* of worship as performed by

---

16. *dhikr* (A) The remembrance of God.

  tasbīh (A) The glorification of God.

  'ibādat (A) Worship and service to the one God.

true wisdom, in accordance with the true meaning of *Īmān-Islām.* One who understands its meaning, its truth, and its reason is in the state of *Īmān-Islām.*

When man glorifies God at the fifth *waqt,* in the universe of the soul, when he worships the Soul of the soul, he is fulfilling an obligatory duty for the *dhāt* [God's essence] and an obligatory duty for an *insān kāmil* of *Īmān-Islām.* Understanding it is also a necessary duty.

It is important to understand these five outer duties, but there are also six inner duties. These must be observed when one stands in the universe of the soul and glorifies the One who is the Soul of the soul.

The first inner duty: When the glorification, or *tasbīh*, reaches Allah and resonates, one will hear with the inner ear of *īmān* the glorification done by Allah, the resonance of His worship, and His responses to the sounds of the worship performed by all the creations in the manifest universe and the unseen divine realms of *'ālam* and *arwāh.* One will hear the words of comfort He offers all lives, the sound of His limitless words and abundant replies, and the sound of His patience and tolerance as He advises all lives. Hearing this with the ear within the ear, the ear of *īmān*, he will savor it saying, "Ah, ah, ah! There is no taste sweeter than this." Thus when one glorifies God, he hears God with his ear of *īmān* and savors the sweetness of those sounds.

The second inner duty: Instead of looking at what one sees with this outer eye, one will look with the inner eye of *īmān*, the eye of light and wisdom which is called *Nūr Muhammadiyyah.* This eye of the wisdom of God's essence, the eye of the form of the *kalimah* known as *Ahamad* and of the beauty of the resplendent countenance known as *Muhammad,* will be overjoyed as bliss beyond bliss when it sees God, His companions, His representatives, the *qutbs,* the archangels, the angels, the praises of all His creations, and the worship that they offer Him. Joyously it will praise Him saying, "Ah, ah, ah!"

The third inner duty: After perceiving His praise, the nose within the nose will inhale the fragrances that emanate there, the jasmine, *kātham kasthūri*, *mullai*, *maru kolundu*, and *savvāthu.*[17] The immeasurable fra-

17. *kātham kasthūri* (T) Fragrant musk; the fragrance associated with the Prophet Muhammad.
mullai (T) Arabian jasmine.
maru kolundu (T) A fragrant shrub with small fragrant leaves.
savvāthu (T) Perfume of a civet cat.

grances of His grace, His *rahmat*, will be inhaled by this nose of *īmān*, and when it perceives the fragrance of the grace of the Lord, it will be overjoyed and say, "Ah, ah, ah, ah!" To be intoxicated by that fragrance and savor that fragrance is the third inner duty.

The fourth inner duty: All beings praise and glorify the Lord, who stands in the universe of the soul as the Soul of the soul. And He gives them the revelations, sounds, resonances, and explanations which are the immeasurable and incomparable beneficent blessings of grace, the honey of grace for all the universes. To bow in reverence, to listen to His words and resonances, to converse with them with the tongue of *īmān*, and to surrender completely to Him and His words is the fourth inner duty.

The fifth inner duty: Having perceived His blissful speech, one should discard the food connected with hunger, old age, disease, and death, and accept the *rizq*, the food that transforms his life into eternal life, or *hayāt*. This food, which comes from the tongue of His essence of grace, should be taken blissfully onto the tongue of *īmān* and tasted with the teeth of light, the teeth of wisdom which are the mercy and compassion of all the universes, the *rahmatul-'ālamīn*. To bring the soul to eternal life, these radiant teeth of divine luminous wisdom, laughing in bliss, should chew on this food, relishing it all the while. They should enjoy the taste of this food that transforms life into a life without birth or death. Laughing in enjoyment and with contentment, they should taste and eat this food that has no hunger, old age, disease, or death. Man must imbibe this food which will totally and perfectly transform his life, making it eternal and death-less.

The sixth inner duty: The *Thiru Marai* known as *Ahamad* is the *Thiru Qur'ān*. Using the twenty-seven letters of the essence of the *kalimah*, one must hand over the innermost heart, the *qalb* called *Ahamad*, and communicate directly with Allah through the revelations that resonate from the *Thiru Qur'ān*, the *Thiru Marai*. That is the state of *Ahamad*, God's essence, His *dhāt*. Thus it is *Ahamad* that communes directly with Allah. This is the sixth inner duty.

These are the five and six duties of an *insān kāmil* of *Īmān-Islām*. May God grant His grace to the followers of *Ahamad* and to those with the beauty of the *Īmān-Islām* of *Muhammad. Āmīn.*

Let us examine further the *Thiru Marai*, the *Thiru Qur'ān*, the *Sūratul-Insān*,[18] and the *Sūratul-Fātihah*.

Sūratul-Fātihah, or the Opening Chapter:[19]

1. *Bismillāhir-Rahmānir-Rahīm.*
   In the name of God, Most Gracious, Most Merciful.

2. *Al-hamdu lillāhi Rabbil-'ālamīn;*
   Praise be to God,
   The Cherisher and Sustainer of the Worlds;

3. *Ar-Rahmānir-Rahīm;*
   Most Gracious, Most Merciful;

4. *Māliki yaumid-dīn.*
   Master of the Day of Judgment.

5. *Iyyāka na'budu wa iyyāka nasta'īn.*
   Thee do we worship,
   And Thine aid we seek.

6. *Ihdinas-sirātal-mustaqīm,*
   Show us the straight way,

7. *Sirātal-ladhīna an'amta 'alaihim,*
   Ghairil-maghdūbi 'alaihim wa lad-dāllīn.
   The way of those on whom
   Thou hast bestowed Thy Grace,
   Those whose (portion)
   Is not wrath,
   And who go not astray.

The meanings of this *sūrat*, or chapter, are limitless. Here is a small explanation.

The twenty-eight Arabic letters comprise the subtle body of man, and each one embodies a quality or an action of God. The ninety-nine holy

---

18. *Sūratul-Insān* (A) The form, or body, of man. Man's physical body is formed of the five elements, but the inner subtle body is composed of the twenty-eight letters of the Arabic alphabet. The *Thiru Qur'ān*, including the 6,666 *āyāt*, is contained and compressed within these letters. See Appendix: *The Twenty-eight Letters within Man: Explanation and Illustrations*, p. 87.

19. *Sūratul-Fātihah* (A) This is the Yusuf Ali translation of the *Sūratul-Fātihah*, The Opening Chapter of the Holy Qur'ān. Bawa Muhaiyaddeen instructed that this be included in the text along with Yusuf Ali's extensive commentary, which can be found in the Appendix, p. 103.

names of God and the *wilāyāt*[20] of God have been set in the body in this way.

Bismillāhir-Rahmānir-Rahīm: He is the Creator, the Protector, and the Nourisher.

Al-hamdu lillāhi: All praise is to Him.

Rabbil-ʿālamīn: Lord of all the universes

Ar-Rahmān: There is nothing like God.

Ar-Rahīm: There is no equal to Him. He cannot be imagined by comparing Him to anything else. There is nothing comparable or equal to Him. He is God. He is the One who protects all lives.

Māliki yaumid-dīn: The word *mālik* means king. He is the king of all the universes. He is the judge to all lives. He is the king of kings for heavenly beings, sages, magicians, kings, divinely wise men, poets, beggars—for all beings. He is the king of all kings. He is the divinely wise to all who are divinely wise. The word *dīn* refers to purity of perfection. He is perfection. He protects and nourishes all lives. He is the purest of the pure to all lives. *Dīn*, in Tamil, is *saivam* or purity.

Iyyākka naʿbudu: He is the One who gives to each of His creations whatever it needs, without selfishness and without seeking the help of others. He gives to all in equal proportion. He does not desire anything, but to those who have desires He gives what is desired. He is pure. He understands right and wrong and gives accordingly. He accepts only what is right. He does not accept anything wrong. He gives what is good to those who want good. He discards that which is evil.

Wa iyyāka nastaʿīn: No matter what they do, He gives to everyone. No one else can give anything to others. He has brought forth the creations, and, understanding very clearly the destiny of each individual, He gives them whatever is needed. He understands their birth and death, their beginning and end, and, having understood, gives accordingly. He is the One who creates correctly, protects correctly, and dispenses justice correctly. He understands the heart

---

20. *wilāyāt* (A) The powers of the qualities with which God performs His duties.

and stomach of all beings and feeds them accordingly. None other than He can feed His creations.

Ihdinas-sirātal-mustaqīm: He understands good and evil with exactitude. He has created right and wrong within good and evil [*khair* and *sharr*]. He has manifested grace and from it brought forth the creation. He has revealed the explanation of the heavens and the hells. He has created the wisdom that can cross the bridge called *sirātal-mustaqīm,* or the straight path. He has placed within man the world governed by a destiny. He has placed grace within man. He has created good and evil within man. He has created earth within man. He has created fire within man, as well as the fire of the light of divine wisdom. He has created water within man, as well as the ocean of *māyā,* and He has created the honey of divine wisdom in the *zamzam*[21] spring that is within man. He has created the air of the evil qualities, as well as the air of the light of the soul. He has created the mind as an aspect of ether and placed the many colors of ether within the mind. He has created His church, which is the innermost heart, known as the *dhāhuth,* the station of *'arsh,*[22] the universe in which He is king. He has also created the hells and the heavens and has inscribed upon His creations, at the time of their creation, that a place in heaven awaits those able to escape the fire of hell.

Sirātal-ladhīna: As the Father of wisdom, God has made a completely perfect place in the church of God for those who are pure, those who have crossed over this fire and this hell and transcended it, those who have crossed the bridge.

An'amta: All the creations created by Allah are His wonders. He is the God to whom the praise of *al-hamdu lillāh* is due. Everything He has created exists within Him, and all control is His.

'Alaihim: He is the king to whom all praise is due. He is the

---

21. *zamzam* (A) A spring near where the *Ka'bah* stands today, which began to gush forth, originally, for Ishmael ☺ and his mother, Hagar ⌣. It is said to flow from the spring of *kauthar* [abundance] in paradise. Here Bawa Muhaiyaddeen is referring to the wellspring of Allah's grace in the throat of man, which never runs dry, is ever full, and gives an exquisite taste which never changes.

22. *Dhāhuth* (Persian) Throne.
    'arsh (A) The throne of Allah; the plenitude from which He rules.

One who has rightfully created, protected, and nourished, the One who dispenses justice to every creation. He is One. God. Allah. He is the only One.

Ghairil: He gives whatever is right to those who ask.

Maghdūbi: He exists as the king who bestows the crown of the kingdom that cannot be estimated, the crown of wisdom and grace.

'Alaihim wa lad-dāllīn: He is the king who has completely destroyed and discarded satan and all his evil and all the fires of hell. Nothing can be compared to God.

God's ninety-nine powers, His *wilāyāt*, exist within you. They exist as the letters that constitute your form. They are the verses that are His attributes or powers. These ninety-nine divine names are what you are. When you have completely understood these ninety-nine names, then Allah alone will remain. When you hand over the ninety-nine powers and give all praise to Him, the praise of *al-hamdu lillāh*, then you will be nothing, and only Allah will exist. This will be the one-hundredth name. He will be as Himself, existing as His own power [*wilāyat*]. At that point only His resonance will be heard. You will not be. One in that state has become Allah.

The letters written in our bodies are expressed outwardly in the *Al-hamdu Sūrat*[23] of the *Qur'ān*. These are His attributes and are called the *asmā'ul-husnā*, or the beautiful names of God. *Insān* [man] himself is the *asmā'ul-husnā* and possesses the powers of the ninety-nine attributes. When he comes to understand these within himself, he will be Allah. He cannot be called *insān* until he understands the attributes of God and the resonance of His divine names. Until then, his understanding will not be that of an *insān*. This is how it is. This is how God's attributes have been revealed in the *Qur'ān*. Every word in the *Qur'ān* has countless meanings.

Sūratul-Ikhlās, or Purity of Faith,[24]

1. *Qul: Huwallāhu ahad;*

---

23. *Al-hamdu Sūrat* (A) The chapter of praise, another name for the opening chapter of the Holy Qur'an, the *Sūratul-Fātihah*.

24. *Sūratul-Ikhlās* [or *Sūrat Ikhlās*] (A) This is the Yusuf Ali translation of *Sūratul-Ikhlās* or Purity of Faith, the CXII Chapter of the Holy Qur'an. Bawa Muhaiyaddeen instructed that this be included in the text along with Yusuf Ali's extensive commentary, which can be found in the Appendix, p. 103.

Say: He is God,
The One and Only;

2. *Allāhus-samad;*
God, the Eternal, Absolute;

3. *Lam yalid, wa lam yūlad;*
He begetteth not,
Nor is He begotten;

4. *Wa lam yakul-lahu kufuwan ahad.*
And there is none
Like unto Him.

This *sūrat* has many meanings. The following is a small explanation of a few of these meanings:

Qul: Huwallāhu ahad: Everything exists as His path of *ahad.*[25] One should understand this *sūrat* and the *Sūratul-Fātihah*, and also the creations which are the mystery, the *ahad*, of *Qul: Huwallāhu ahad.* Understanding this is *Īmān-Islām.* If one is an *insān kāmil* he will understand this *ahad*, this mystery, which is the completeness within Allah, and His resonance to *qul hū*,[26] to all of everything. He will understand this *sūrat.*

Allāhus-samad: Everything is in a state of equality within Him. This is His field of justice. It exists as His truth for all lives and for everything. He is the One who gives the food. He is the One who hears, the One who knows the heart and decides, the One who calls us back. He is clarity and love. He is the One who understands what heaven is, the One who rules as the good ruler. *Allāhus-samad.* Existing in all lives in a state of equality, Allah is the One who is the peacefulness and the equality which treats everything equally. Holding other lives as equal to His own life, understanding and accepting the energy of all lives, He is the One who gives the meanings, the One who has created patience, tolerance, and peacefulness, the One who is justice. *Allāhus-samad* is the raised flag of purity, of *dīn,*

---

25. *Ahad* (A) One of the ninety-nine names of Allah. The only One; the secret One who is a mystery. See *Asmā'ul-Husnā: The 99 Beautiful Names of Allah* by M. R. Bawa Muhaiyaddeen. In this context, it is used to mean the mystery or the secret of unity.

26. *qul hū* (A) Bawa Muhaiyaddeen puns on the word *qul hū. Kullahu* means 'everything'.

the flag that rules. He is the One without selfishness. He exists as the able One, the One who rules as king before and after, the One who always decides. He is the One who exists forever and ever.

Lam yalid: The story of the One of grace who is within all of everything. To the poor, He will be poor. To the slave, He will be a slave. To the humble, He will be humble. To the learned, He will be learned. To the great, He will be great. To purity, He will be purity. To a king, He will be a king. To a beggar, He will be a beggar. *Yalid.* He lives in the left breath and in the right. He exists forever in the left side and in the right side. *Lam yalid* is the *Nūr* which is the light that rules in the *qalb*, the innermost heart. He rules in the *qalb* in that state. He is the One who has clarity. He is the perfect One, the knowing One.

Lam yalid, wa lam yūlad: He is the One who is always there as the purity in the heart. He is the One who makes things understandable and clear, the One who corrects everything, the One who makes the decisions, the One who is tolerant. He is the One who will exist within forever, the One who will give the grace in the universe of the souls, the One who will bring the souls forth, the One who will create lives. *Lam yalid.* He is the One who is humble to His devotees. He is a slave to His slaves. He will be eminent to the eminent. He exists as *lam yalid* and *wa lam yūlad.*

Wa lam yūlad: Among beneficial things, He understands that which is within truth, that which is on the right side, that which is within the perfection of the resplendence of the *Nūr. Wa lam yūlad:* He exists as the everlasting truth and as the powerful One within all who are righteous. He exists on the right side within *illallāhu.* He exists within the light of the *Nūr.* He exists as the One who helps. He is the everlasting powerful One and exists within us as a power. He is within the truth as the resplendence of the *Nūr.* He is the One who is within purity. He exists as the purity within *īmān,* as the plenitude within the purity, as the power within Allah's grace, as the power within the power. He exists within the wealth which does not diminish. He exists within His qualities, within those who have His qualities. *Wa lam yūlad:* He is the One within, who will exist forever in the pure *qalb*—that is *wa lam yūlad.*

Wa lam yakul-lahu: He is the One who is always within, in all of everything, to all of everything, as the omnipresent plenitude. He will exist within forever. He is the One who understands the meanings. He is the One who is known as *Allāhu.* He is the One who is the resonance.

Kufuwan ahad: He is the *ahad*, the mystery, to all of everything. To the eighteen thousand universes He exists as the secret beauty. He knows and accepts all of the explanations. To know Him and worship Him on the secret path is to know Him as the secret on that secret path. He is the secret. He is the grace. He exists as the concealed One, as the mystery. He is the mystery within the mystery. He exists as wisdom within wisdom. He is the One who exists unseen by the mind or by desire, the One who exists unseen by the things of the body and the world. He is the One who exists without form, without anything. He exists alone on the secret path, existing without the aspect of wrong on the path known as right and wrong. He exists as the truth within rightness in the creations who have right and wrong. On the path of the essence, the *dhāt*, He exists as grace. He dwells in this state as the *sirr*, the secret of creation.

He exists as the mystery, as the secret, as the *ahad*. He is the One who knows and understands with wisdom. He must be recognized as the secret. The One who is the secret must be understood through the secret. *Allāhu.* That is the wisdom of the secret path, a place which mind and desire cannot reach. The *Nūr* stands within, going within and within the within, going in and cutting ninety-nine times and merging within, cutting with His qualities and going beyond, going within as the quality within the quality, going within as the duty within the duty, going within as the action within the action, going within as the heart within the heart, going within as the *ahad*, or mystery, within the *ahad*.

Know Him as you go within. Know that other than Allah there is no one else. Realize that secret. The secret which is concealed within the *ahad* is *Allāhu*—the hidden meaning, the endless meaning. *Allāhu.* Only He is *Allāhu*. Nothing else is. Understanding that and going within is the meaning of *ahad*. The path of *ahad* is purity. Purity is the meaning of the *ahad*. This is Allah's *Sūratul-Ikhlās*, along with a brief explanation. It has to be understood. One who knows and understands this path and acts with God's qualities is *Īmān-Islām, insān kāmil.* He belongs to the one group among the seventy-three groups, the group of *Nūr Muhammadiyyah.*

An *insān kāmil* of *Īmān-Islām* should understand this. This is the explanation contained in the *Qur'ān,* the *Thiru Marai,* which explains the meaning of the *kalimah* being formed of twenty-seven letters and *Īmān-Islām* having twenty-eight, of the *insān kāmil* who is *Īmān-Islām,* and of the *Ahamad-Muhammad* which is *Īmān-Islām.*

The 6,666 verses which carry this explanation are contained within the *Qur'ān.* And this explanation is buried within the form of the *kalimah* that is within *insān.* It is the resonance of Allah's essence known as *Ahamad,* and the explanation of the beauty of Allah's countenance known as *Muhammad.* That which understands this is the resplendence of *Īmān-Islām.* One who understands this is the resplendence of wisdom known as *insān kāmil,* the resplendence of *Nūr Muhammad.*

Now let us speak more about the duties. According to these duties, there are four steps in worship. We have been speaking about the first of these four, the worship of an *insān kāmil* who is *Īmān-Islām.* We will discuss the other three a little later.

To those who have the absolute certitude of faith known as *īmān,* there is nothing they hold precious other than the Lord, the *Rabb.* There is nothing else for them. Such is the perfection and completeness of their *īmān.* However for *Īmān-Islām,* five and six duties have been pointed out:

First, to believe in Allah with certitude.
Second, prayer.
Third, charity and tithe [*sadaqah* and *zakat*].
Fourth, fasting.
Fifth, *hajj,* or holy pilgrimage.

This *hajj* is for those who have the means, those who seek and hoard the wealth of the world, the wages and the rewards of the world, those who make the world their own and rule it, those who use their desires and mind to amass the world for themselves. These five duties have been given to those who rule the world and have complete faith in the world.

Let us further explain the first and second duties. It is the duty of every one of Allah's creations to worship Allah, to pray to Him, to believe in Him and know Him; to believe with certainty that there is no other God responsible for creation and protection; to have the certitude of *īmān* that all of everything is His kingdom—*awwal, dunyā,* and *ākhirah,* including the eighteen thousand universes; to understand that there is none equal to Him; to attain the *īmān,* the faith and certitude, that He has no beginning or end; to accept that He is the One who creates without any flaw, that He is the One able to protect the body, life, earth, sky, good, evil, heaven, and hell; and to accept that He is the only One who gives judgment on Judgment Day.

Thus it is the duty of all His creations to attain the certitude and *īmān* that there is no other who creates, provides food, protects, and gives judgment. It is the duty of all creations and *insān* to accept with total determination that there is none other than *Allāhu ta'ālā* who is worthy of worship; to worship only Him without considering anything else as equal to Him, or worshiping anything else in place of Him; and to accept Him determinedly and without the slightest doubt as the One who has no equal and is incomparable and limitless.

Worshiping Him with a knowledge of this is the duty of every individual. This is the most important of all duties. It is the path of His commandments. This truth must be known to everyone. It was for those who did not accept this duty in the proper manner, that the five commandments were sent down to the *Rasūl* ﷺ.

First, one must have certitude and faith in Allah. Second, one must worship Him. The third commandment of charity [*sadaqah*] was given for those who did not understand that all of everything, even the body and soul, belongs to Allah. Because they did not understand this or have certitude of faith in Him and instead gathered the things of the world to themselves—in order that they might learn to perform charity and good deeds, they were told, "At least do this. Follow this commandment. Since you have gathered My possessions, claiming them as yours, you must share them with others."

And for those who could not fulfill the duty of charity properly, for those whose *īmān* was even less than this, the fourth commandment of fasting was given. They were told, "At least understand that your hunger is the same as another's hunger and that your sorrow is the same as another's sorrow. Feel your hunger, and through it realize what another's hunger is like. Understand another's suffering through your own suffering." It was to make people experience and understand this that the fourth obligatory duty, the commandment of fasting, was given.

And for those who did not understand fasting and did not know the meaning of *īmān*, determination, and God's treasures, the fifth duty was ordained, the holy pilgrimage, or *hajj*. The people were told, "Go on *hajj*. Wear the robes that look like a burial shroud and fulfill this duty as though you were a corpse. Before leaving, distribute all your wealth. If you have a wife and children, give your wife the dowry that is due to her, and give the children their share. Distribute what is left among your relatives and the poor. Then, in a state of death, fulfill this fifth duty. People with wealth and money should fulfill it in Mecca. Those who do not have the means can fulfill the *hajj* by attending the congregational prayers every Friday [*jum'ah*]. In this way, *hajj* has been made *halāl*, or lawful, for you fifty-two times a year, and you should fulfill that." Thus, a different way of fulfilling this duty has been pointed out for those without wealth.

For those who do not understand these five duties, six others were established as exhortations, to help people attain *īmān* and make them realize God. Only if you understand these six duties will your *īmān* dawn.

1. Believe in Allah.
2. Believe in His angels.
3. Believe in His books (scriptures).
4. Believe in His prophets.
5. Believe in the Day of Judgment.
6. Believe in the Lord who created good and bad and placed them within you. You should understand both and act in accordance with that understanding, for tomorrow He will inquire into your good and bad and give you an appropriate place. You should realize who is the Master and Emperor, the One who will know whether you have acted with understanding. You must believe in Him. You must believe that He is God.

If one understands the first five duties, then he is Islam. Allah has said, "*Yā Muhammad*, I created everything through you. Everything created is Islam." If one understands this, he is Islam, or purity, even if he is not born a Muslim. But only after he understands the last six duties, which are cautionary in nature, does he truly have *īmān*. If one understands them and accepts that Allah is the only One, if he accepts that all of everything belongs to Allah and surrenders to Him, only then will the state of *īmān* be established in him. If one understands these commandments of God and realizes the grace and strength of *īmān*, he will join the one group out of the seventy-three groups among mankind. If, however, he does not understand this, he will join the other seventy-two groups. If he does not understand even the seventy-two groups and join them, he will be caught in satan's group. His lord will be satan.

Since everyone was born Islam [pure], they should reflect upon this and understand these duties. One who has attained *īmān* by reflecting upon, understanding, and realizing them will be one of *Īmān-Islām, dīnul-Islām*.

We have spoken about the five and six duties pertaining to the seventy-two groups and their levels of faith. Earlier we spoke about the one group with the certitude of *īmān*, the group of *insān kāmil*. Now, we will give three other explanations, explanations concerning three types of *dhikr*. We will discuss the worship done in each: *adh-dhikrul-jalī* [in which the sound is heard externally], *adh-dhikrul-qalbī* [remembrance by the inner heart], and *adh-dhikrur-rūhī* [remembrance by the soul].

Amongst all the worship known as *'ibādat*, the resonances of the *dhikr* are the ones that reach up to the *'arsh*, or throne of Allah. But the *dhikr* known as *adh-dhikrul-jalī* reaches out for the world. It arises from the fervor of the *nafs*, the cravings and base desires in the mind and emerges resonating as a loud sound. This sound arises from the fervor of the angels that represent the five elements: earth, fire, water, air, and ether. It is the *dhikr* of the angels and the base desires. This *dhikrul-jalī* relates to the intentions of the world, to cravings, the mind, and to base desires. It continually reaches out to grasp the world.

The *dhikr* of the innermost heart [*adh-dhikrul-qalbī*] is performed by those who have attained the state of *'arshul-mu'min*,[27] for Allah dwells within the mosque that is in their innermost heart. The beauty of that is *Muhammad*, which is the beauty of the countenance of Allah. It is called *Nūr Muhammadiyyah*. It is the resonance of the essence of Allah. *Ahamad* is the heart, the *qalb*, the essence of Allah. It is the Messenger of Allah.

---

27. *'arshul-mu'min* (A) The heart of a true believer is a throne for God.

The *dhikr* of the *qalb* is the one by which that Messenger speaks directly with God. Thus the *dhikr* of the *qalb* is the *dhikr* of *mi'rāj*. Drawing the 6,666 verses from within the grace of *īmān*, this *dhikr* communes with Allah within the *qalb* called *'arshul-mu'min*. This communion with Allah, the *dhikr* of the *qalb*, is performed by the divine luminous wisdom known as *Nūr Muhammad*. It is a *dhikr* that reaches up to the *dhāhuth*, the throne of Allah.

The third *dhikr* is the *dhikr* done by the soul, *adh-dhikrur-rūhī*. The soul, the *rūh*, is a ray that came from God, from His power. *Lā ilāha illallāhu wa innī 'Īsā Rūhullāh*: Nothing other than God exists. You alone are God. Jesus is the soul of God, and there will be another prophet. The soul has eternal life. It has no shadow. It has no end. It has no darkness. It is not affected by torpor or hypnotic fascination. It has neither form nor subtle form. Allah and the soul are of the same nature—the nature of His essence, or *dhāt*. The soul has no night or day. It has no death or birth. That soul, which is perfection, communes with Allah, who is the Soul of the soul, the *Rūh* of the *rūh*. Thus the soul does *dhikr* to the Soul. The divine luminous wisdom known as the *Nūr* merges with the soul and becomes its light. This light worships and does *dhikr* to Allah, reaching up to His *'arsh*, which is His place of justice, and intermingles with Allah and the *mubārakāt* [His state of sovereignty for all three worlds], His *dhāhuth*, or throne, His church, and His kingdom known as *rahmatul-'ālamīn*. This *dhikr* of the soul intermingles with God and merges with Him in a state of oneness. It is the *dhikr* in which duality ceases to exist and both become one. It is performed by one who is merged with Allah. On the other hand, those who do the *adh-dhikrul-jalī*, are performing a *dhikr* that intermingles with the world and base desires. That *dhikr* is connected to the world.

Thus *dhikr* can be done in these three forms. When one does the *dhikr* of the inner heart [*qalb*] and the *dhikr* of the soul [*rūh*], he knows no day or night. These two *dhikrs* communicate directly with Allah and go on unceasingly. These *dhikrs* exist within Him, glorifying and worshiping Him. The *insān kāmils* who are performing the *dhikr* of the *qalb* have become the *'arshul-mu'mins* of *Allāhu*. They are performing a *dhikr* that always keeps God in their *qalb*. This means that their *qalb* is the mosque in which Allah dwells, that Allah Himself has come to reside in the temple of their *qalb*.

Each child must understand this and perform it in the right manner. For those who do this *dhikr*, there is no treasure other than God. There is no kingdom other than the kingdom of Allah. There is no grace other than the grace of Allah and no love other than Allah's love. There is no sustenance other than the sustenance of Allah's grace. There is no intention other than the intention for Allah. There is no worship other than the worship of Allah, no praise other than the praise of Allah. There is no yearning other than the yearning for Allah. There is no wealth other than the wealth of Allah's grace. There is no bliss other than that of Allah. There is no love or praise other than Allah's praise or love. *Al-hamdu lillāh* [all praise belongs to God]. Everything is His praise, everything is His story.

This is the worship and *dhikr* performed by an *insān kāmil* who has attained perfect certitude of *īmān* in Allah. For such a person, everything other than Allah is hostile to him. Everything he sees, everything he perceives—his mind, his desire, his vision, his relationships, attachments, race, caste, scriptures, and religions—all will oppose him. Allah is the only One who rightfully belongs to him, the only One who is precious to him. Allah is his only wealth for all three worlds. Allah is the only Lord who protects and sustains. For an *insān kāmil* nothing else exists. Every manifested thing is his enemy.

Therefore, my children, realize this truth and accept without the slightest doubt the ways in which the worship of Allah should be done. When one is in this state of *dhikr*, the soul functions constantly with no difference between day and night. The *qalb* which is Allah's grace, the light known as *Ahamad*, His essence, resplends night and day; the effulgent divine luminous wisdom known as *Nūr Muhammad* resonates within and converses with Allah continuously; the revelations of Allah constantly descend into the form of Allah's *kalimah*; and the beauty of Allah's countenance continuously resplends and shines in the face known as *Muhammad*, worshiping Allah without limit, day and night. You should try to attain and establish this state. You should try to make this worship be your worship. You must make this *dhikr* and prayer your *dhikr* and prayer. If you establish this state, Allah will give you His perfect beauty and His wealth, the wealth of the three worlds. May He grace you with these things. May He gather you to His place and join you with Him so that both are one. *Āmīn*.

Understand this and do it in this way. This is prayer, or *vanakkam*. This is perfect prayer. Accept this prayer, accept Him, accept His *Ahamad*, accept the beauty of His countenance that is His *Nūr*, accept the treasure of the twenty-seven letters of His *kalimah* which arise from His essence, or *dhāt*, and converse with Him. Accept the twenty-eight letters of the *Qur'ān* known as *īmān*. Understand that this is the *Ummul-Qur'ān*.[28] Understand the 6,666 verses in it, the 124,000 prophets of God, the angels and archangels, the *qutbs*, His wonders, His grace, His essence, and everything else. Listen to the meanings that are explained; listen to the resonance glorifying Him. Dwell in communion with Him and worship in this way. This will be the *dhikr* and worship that reaches Him. *Āmīn, Yā Rabbal-'ālamīn:* May these be fulfilled, O Ruler of the universes.

May His praise fall upon all of you. May His qualities dawn within your *qalb*. Without ever letting go of your hand, may He embrace you to His *qalb*, absorb you into His essence, or *dhāt*, known as *Ahamad*, and bestow His grace upon you. *Āmīn*.

This is the worship in the prayer of *Īmān-Islām*, known as *dīnul-Islām*. Allah's *Rasūl* ﷺ has explained this according to the level of each one's wisdom. As soon as your wisdom has attained completion, you will see that this is the only *dhikr* that will reach Him. Understand this and follow this. *Āmīn, Yā Rabbal-'ālamīn*. May this be fulfilled, O Ruler of the universes.

May 18, 1974

---

28. *Ummul-Qur'ān:* (A) The 'source' or 'mother' of the *Qur'ān;* the mother of man's wisdom, justice, and faith; the mother who raises the true believer.

CHAPTER TWO

With Every Breath

Bawa Muhaiyaddeen points to his big toe and says:

*I*f an ant were to crawl on one's toe, its movement would be experienced through one's feeling [*unarvu*] and awareness [*unarchi*].[1] Similarly, the movement of the *dhikr* should be distinguished using the different levels of wisdom. Just as feeling perceives the crawling of an ant on your skin, it should perceive the movement of the *dhikr* as you draw it up from the toes, saying, "*Lā ilāha*." Awareness should locate where the *dhikr* begins. And, just as intellect [*pudthi*] recognizes what is crawling, it should also identify the power that is the *dhikr*. The intellect should draw this *dhikr*, which flows along with the words *lā ilāha*. While intellect is pulling, feeling and awareness must join with it and move along. You must be aware of all this in the same way that one is aware of an ant crawling on the body.

As the *dhikr* moves along, assessment [*mathi*] should be controlling its flow. Acting as a brake, assessment determines where to halt the *dhikr* and where to let it flow. While assessment controls the flow of the *dhikr*, subtle wisdom [*arivu*] monitors it and identifies the areas in which it is functioning at each moment. Just as feeling, awareness, and intellect inform you that an ant is creeping here, crawling there, scratching here, or biting there, similarly feeling, awareness, intellect, assessment, and subtle wisdom should check on the movement of the *dhikr* and make you aware of its flow.

As subtle wisdom monitors its flow, you will be aware of its movement in all the skin pores, all the nerves and blood vessels, and throughout the flesh.[2] When its sound falls on the nerves (which are similar to

---

1. What is called wisdom is not a simple thing. There are seven levels of wisdom, or states of consciousness, innate in a human being: feeling [*unarvu*], awareness [*unarchi*], intellect [*pudthi*], assessment or judgment [*mathi*], subtle wisdom [*arivu*], divine analytic or discerning wisdom [*pahuth arivu*], and divine luminous wisdom [*perr arivu*]. See Appendix: *The Seven Levels of Consciousness*, p. 109 and Glossary.

2. Bawa Muhaiyaddeen, in answer to a question, explained, "Yes, you will feel its movement, but only

the strings of a *vīna*),[3] its music is heard by the ears and the inner heart, or *qalb*. This has to be known by feeling, awareness, intellect, assessment, and subtle wisdom. You should focus on this sound heard by these five levels of wisdom. As soon as the *dhikr* rises up and enters the heart, assessment halts it there, while divine analytic wisdom [*pahuth arivu*], saying, "Other than You," separates that sound from the breath and hears it.

Bawa Muhaiyaddeen demonstrates, sitting cross-legged, erect, no particular posture, both hands extended forward (slightly closed and facing downward) with both wrists resting on the knees.

The eyebrows, hairs, breath, mouth, and tongue ... all experience the movement of the *dhikr*, and the tip of the tongue flutters as if it were playing a flute. There, as each level of consciousness unfolds, the wisdom of awareness must split off this sound of the *dhikr* from the breath. Just as a flutist, with the tip of his tongue, directs the air in a way that will bring forth the melody he has in mind, you must, with a gentle trill of the tip of your tongue (not moving it too much up or down) blow on this inner 'flute', separating off the sound of *lā ilāha:* There is nothing other than You, O Lord. This thought, or remembrance, must do the separating and pass that sound along. Feeling must separate it and pass it along. Awareness must separate it and pass it along. Intellect must separate it and pass it along. Assessment must separate it and pass it along. Subtle wisdom must identify it and separate it and pass it along. Finally divine analytic wisdom must separate that sound of *lā ilāha:* Other than You there is no Lord. As the breath rises with this sound, the *dhikr* must rise up to the *'arsh* [crown of the head, the throne of God].

Question: Does it go inward?

Bawa Muhaiyaddeen: Accompanied by *lā ilāha*, the breath flows upward from below, does it not?

As it rises there will be a fluttering of the left eyelid, causing the breath to split off. With the word *lā ilāha*, with a glance of the eye and a quiver of the lips, nose, eyebrows, and forehead, the *dhikr* is drawn up to the *'arsh*. Here it is separated from the breath by divine analytic wisdom with

---

when subtle wisdom, the fifth level of wisdom, comes into play. This takes time and practice. Do you not have to make the tip of the thread sharp before you can thread it through the eye of a needle? That is how it is." From 6/2/74 audio tape 7404-21.

3. *vīna* (T) A lute from India, usually of seven strings and two octaves, which may be compared with the seven levels of consciousness and the incoming and outgoing breaths.

the sound of *lā ilāha:* There is none other than You. The breath is then drawn down and pushed out (through the left nostril) with the thought, "Go away." It must ride out on that sound, that vibration, which is wisdom.

As soon as the breath has been pushed out through the left nostril and inhalation begins through the right nostril, there will be a slight movement of the right eyelid, or right side of the forehead, or right eyebrow, or right nostril, or the lips. With this movement, divine analytic wisdom should point to the *Nūr*, the light of God. Although the *Nūr* is within everything, filling everything, divine analytic wisdom should now point to it, to God.

Subtle wisdom must perceive this, just as awareness earlier perceived how the *lā ilāha* came up from below. That same awareness must now attach itself to the *Nūr* [light of God] while saying, "*Illallāhu.*" Feeling must also grasp it, intention [*niyyat*] must grasp it, intellect must grasp it, and assessment must grasp it and control it. Subtle wisdom must grasp it. Divine analytic wisdom must grasp it, saying, "There is none other than You. You alone are God." Having grasped it, divine analytic wisdom must pull it along saying, "*Illallāhu,*" and, with a trembling of the right forehead, draw it in through the right nostril and install it in the inner heart [*qalb*]. This too you should be aware of. Awareness, along with the other levels of wisdom, must attach itself to God, to His light, which is the *Nūr.* Wisdom should be aware of it attaching itself to the light and drawing it along. In the same way that awareness knew how the *lā ilāha* moved and came up from below, it must be aware of this *illallāhu*, grasp it, identify it, and establish it in the right side of the *qalb*. It should be aware of the movement of this weighty word *illallāhu*, as it is being drawn in on the breath through the right nostril. From there it should be taken up to the *kursī* [gnostic eye], at the center of the forehead, between the eyebrows. Here, a heaviness will be felt when the breath is being drawn in.

Indicating the point between the two eyebrows, Bawa Muhaiyaddeen says:

This is the center of divine knowledge [*gnānam*]. It is known as the eye of wisdom. There is light here and also a feeling of heaviness. It is the *dhikr* pausing in this station that causes the heaviness or pressure. When the pressure builds, the *dhikr* goes in through the brain and descends to the back of the tongue, to the throat. You should feel it descending.

At this point the breath should again activate the flute at the tip of the tongue, saying, "*Illallāhu:* You alone are Allah." This is where the sound separates from the breath. Accompanied by that sound, the *dhikr* should move downward to the heart. The vibration here is *illallāhu:* You alone are God! As wisdom affirms this, it must also be aware of the place in the heart where the *dhikr* is being installed.

When the musical sound is being separated and passed along, it will cause the 4,448 blood vessels, the nerves, and the pores of the skin to resonate with the sound *illallāhu:* You alone are God. Just as the strings of a musical instrument vibrate when plucked, bringing forth music, the sound of the vibrations of *illallāhu* will be experienced all over the body, in every nerve and in every hair follicle. However, if at this stage our concentration wavers, if the mind strays from its focus even slightly, we will not experience this. It will not be the *dhikr.* There must be one-pointed concentration of our whole being. Feeling, awareness, intellect, assessment, subtle wisdom, and divine analytic wisdom—these six—along with divine luminous wisdom, should be concentrating one-pointedly on the *dhikr.* All seven levels of wisdom must function as one. Like guards, they should be monitoring its flow. Your heart and your gaze should be focused on that point.

Bawa Muhaiyaddeen explains further:

When you say, "*Lā ilāha,*" these six sections should draw the breath upward from the tips of the toes, in the same way that a pump suctions out the air in order to draw dirty water up from a well. And just as the pump then pushes out that dirty water, the six states of consciousness push out the impure breath with the words *lā ilāha:* Other than You there is nothing. This water belongs to the world and is being pushed out. The remembrance of, "There is nothing but You," draws up all the impurities—all the evil qualities, desires, and *māyā* or illusion—right from the toes. In this way, the energies of our evil qualities and the properties of *māyā* are all drawn up and pushed out into the world where they can nourish the crops of *māyā.* Thus the water within is gradually purified. The motor says, "This water does not belong within you; it belongs outside," and it pumps the impurities out.

When you say, "*Illallāhu:* You alone are Allah," the motor of awareness [*unarchi*] connects that *dhikr* to the light which is the *Nūr* and draws in its current. Using the seven levels of wisdom, you draw God's current from the *Nūr*, then experience it and install the light in the inner heart. The vibrations, the movements of the face, the glance, the wisdom of awareness—all these come into play at this time when that light-power is being drawn along, accompanied by the sound of *illallāhu*. Not only should you be aware of these, as well as the sounds and resonances, you must understand their significance, and also experience the power of that light. When you say, *"illallāhu,"* you need to be aware of the manner in which the light is drawn forth and the way its resplendence fills the *qalb*. You should even perceive that light and feel the power of this current filling the *qalb* and then flowing from there along all the wires throughout your body.

Thus, that which is drawn down from the crown of the head to the heart (on the incoming breath) is a current, whereas that which is drawn up from the toes (on the outgoing breath) is the air of the base desires [*nafs*]. Those base desires are drawn up from the depths of our body on the air and are pushed out. While they are being drawn up and expelled, feeling, awareness, intellect, assessment, subtle wisdom, and divine analytic wisdom combine to check on the various parts of the body from which the base desires are being drawn.

This process works like the passage of air through a flute. Or, like a pump, it uses the breath to draw up the base desires and bring them to the motor, which isolates them and throws them out saying, "Other than God there is nothing else. Go away!" These base desires belong to the five elements (earth, fire, water, air, and ether), and are drawn up and cast out, saying, "God, the One, is real, not you. Go!"

This part of the *dhikr* is conducted through the agency of air. Through the *lā ilāha*, the air of the outgoing breath is used to suck up the gases and vapors of the base desires and expel them. This breath is known as the moon breath [*chandira kalai*].[4] It is one of the sixty-four arts, or *kalais*. Through the *chandira kalai* the gases are drawn up and then thrown out, as you say, "Go away! Nothing exists but God." This is *kalai gnānam*.[5]

---

4. *kalai* (T) Lit. the sixty-four arts and sciences. One of these arts is controlling the breath. Bawa Muhaiyaddeen explains that *sūriya kalai* (sun breath, the breath inhaled on the right side) is the breath of divine analytic wisdom. It is the breath of *qutbiyyat* or light, the breath of divine wisdom. *Chandira kalai* (moon breath, the breath exhaled on the left side) is the breath of the world. It is the breath of the seven colors: earth, fire, water, air, ether, mind, and desire.

5. *kalai gnānam* (T) The wisdom of the sixty-four arts and sciences; universal knowledge; all the learning, poetry, songs, and music of the world.

These impurities are strummed by the *kalai* and pushed out, just as the strings of a stringed instrument are strummed to produce the sound *ting, ting, ting, ting*. The music of the *kalai* draws out the things that belong to earth and pushes them out through the left nostril, saying, "Go away."

The breath drawn in through the right nostril is known as the sun breath [*sūriya kalai*]. It is light. This sun, which is wisdom, should be drawn in by the current of wisdom and taken up to the *Nūr*, which is God's light and plenitude. That which exists as the wisdom within wisdom is Allah. Contact with this wisdom has to be made by divine analytic wisdom. When the contact is made and the power is being drawn forth with the words *illallāhu*, feeling, awareness, intellect, assessment, subtle wisdom, and divine analytic wisdom should all discern which areas of the body the power is being drawn through, just as they did when the *dhikr* was being drawn up from the toes.

In the same way that a voltage tester is used to check the flow of electric current into a light switch, wisdom should be aware of the flow of this current. On the voltage tester, a bulb will glow if the current is flowing. (There are also built-in safety measures to protect the person holding the tester from danger of electrocution.) Just as this instrument detects the flow of electric current, divine luminous wisdom [*perr arivu*, the seventh level of wisdom] makes sure that the current is flowing steadily and verifies what divine analytic wisdom [*pahuth arivu*, the sixth level] is bringing along. It checks to see where the *dhikr* is at each point of time and whether it is reaching each switch—one eye, the other eye, the brain, the *'arsh*—each station. It must touch every switch to make sure. Thus, as the *dhikr* is being drawn forth saying, "*Illallāhu*," divine luminous wisdom must touch each station to see whether the current has reached each location and is descending as it should. All seven levels have to be functioning correctly, monitoring the current accurately as it is being drawn along. They check on the sound, the current, and the light, and finally install the current in the inner heart [*qalb*], saying, "*Illallāhu*: You are God."

Now the current has reached the *qalb*. Once the power reaches that motor and the switch is turned on, the current flows out through all 4,448 blood vessels, and is distributed to the eighteen thousand universes that lie within.

Your inner televisions, radios, telephones, lights, and other things which work on this electric current can now function, and you have instant access to every station within you. If any station malfunctions, you will know at once. If there is a problem in some country, or a breakdown somewhere in any of the factories, a telephone message will be received instantly. Or if there is a war in one of the countries, or heavy rains, gales, or cyclones, you will be able to see it on your inner television instantly and send someone to rectify it.

However, all this can be achieved only if the *dhikr* is done correctly, with one-pointed concentration. There will be no success if you let your focus wander here and there. It will be of no use at all. Only if the senses have been brought under control and the seven states of awareness are functioning in one-pointed concentration can you truly pray.

This is not the focus of the prayers done in temples, churches, or mosques. There you can be alert when you choose. You can let your gaze wander, or you can even be talking to your neighbor during prayer. But in this prayer every aspect of you must be focused on the one point— God—not straying to any other point. Nothing must deviate even the slightest. Your breath, your speech, your sound, the music that comes from your nerves, your blood vessels, and your bones—every one of these must be unswerving in its concentration on the one point. This is the state you have to be in when you are doing the *dhikr*. Then every one of the 43,242 breaths[6] that you take each day will be a prostration [*sajdah*] at the feet of Allah. It is not easy.

Initially, as you begin to practice the *dhikr*, you should concentrate on the process by which, using the breath as a pump, you draw up the un- wanted impurities within you and push them out. All of the bondages we inherited at birth—the five senses which are the trapdoors of illusion, the *karma* of our birth, our faults and sins—all these have to be pumped up and pushed out. These impure waters of the *karma* of our birth must be drawn up from the pit of our birth, the hell from which we were born. Using the breath, the *dhikr* of *lā ilāha* should suck out these foul waters, along with our impure qualities and actions, and send them out saying, "Go away!"

In the *illallāhu* part of this *dhikr*, divine analytic wisdom contacts *Allāhu*,

---

6. Bawa Muhaiyaddeen has explained that: An adult human being usually takes 15 to 16 breaths every minute. Thus he takes 15 to 16 x 60 breaths every hour, and 15 to 16 x 60 x 24 breaths every 24 hours, which equals 21,621 breaths every day. Since each breath consists of an outgoing breath and an incoming breath, a human being may be said to take 43,242 breaths each day.

the power which is wisdom within wisdom, draws it forth as a current, and establishes it as *illallāhu*, which is the light, God. First divine analytic wisdom sifts and removes the unclean substances of birth, *karma*, and *māyā*, and pushes them outside. Saying, *"Lā ilāha:* There is none other than You," it draws up the five elements, along with the aspects of *māyā* connected to them, and expels them. After separating off and discarding all that is unclean, it makes contact with that which is truth, that which is wisdom within wisdom, that which is perfect purity, and draws the current, that power, along with it. As divine analytic wisdom carries this power along, assisted by feeling, awareness, intellect, assessment, and subtle wisdom, the *Nūr*, the light of God, which is divine luminous wisdom, checks to make sure the current is flowing as it should. The *Nūr* keeps checking to see whether the current is flowing properly and reaching the various stations—the nerves, the muscles, skin, bones, and blood. Finally, as you say, *"Illallāhu,"* divine luminous wisdom takes the current safely and deposits it in its final station, the inner heart, the *qalb*.

This *dhikr* can be called true prayer or prostration only when all seven levels of consciousness—feeling, awareness, intellect, assessment, subtle wisdom, divine analytic wisdom, and divine luminous wisdom—are focused one-pointedly to monitor the flow of the power. If the eye wanders somewhere other than that point, the whole thing is lost. If the mind strays, or if feeling, or awareness, or intellect, or assessment, or subtle wisdom stray, it is lost. All seven states of awareness must stay focused. This is the way the *dhikr* must be done.

When one is correctly performing the *dhikr* in this manner, if he is stabbed or shot, he will not know it. The shot will not strike him. The stabbing will not pierce him. Lightning will not strike him.

Question: Will he just not be aware of it, or will it not even touch him?

Bawa Muhaiyaddeen: He will not be aware of it, nor will it touch him, for that state is God. That is, the man is no longer there. Only God is there. At the time that he is experiencing that power, he is as God. When his state of prayer is such, he is God. This is the true state of prayer. If anything were to die at this time, it would be God. Whatever happens to the man at this time happens to God. 'He' no longer exists. There is nothing, only God. Thus, if he has been performing the *dhikr* correctly the blow cannot strike him.

When gasoline comes in contact with fire, it is the gasoline that is burnt up, not the fire. Similarly, when anything falls on that point, it is burnt. When one is in a state of true *dhikr*, any danger that comes toward him will itself be destroyed.

This is *sūfi gnānam*.[7] This is prostration to God, performed 43,242 times each day. This is the state of merging with God, the state of God-man, man-God. In this state man contacts God directly. Only in such a state is it true prayer. It is both *salām* and *salawāt*.[8]

Man gives *salāms* to God directly, "*As-salāmu 'alaikum, Yā Allāhu:* May peace be upon You, O God!" and God replies with the prayer, "*'Alaikumus-salām:* On you too may there be peace."

Man says, "O Merciful One! *Yā Rahmān! Al-hamdu lillāh:* All praise be to You!" and God replies, "*Al-hamdu lillāh:* I give praise to you!" This is true prayer, where man knows God and prays to Him directly, contacting Him at the place where man and God are merged. This is the point.

This *dhikr* is done in two parts: *lā ilāha* and *illallāhu*. Talking about it is easy, but doing it in exactly this way is extremely hard. However, if you do succeed, you will realize the state of man-God, God-man. The 'I' will be nothing. The 'I' will not exist. It will be God worshiping God.

You may ask, "How is it possible for man to become God and God to become man?" But at that point man does not exist, only God is there. As soon as one understands this, he realizes that he is nothing. Man says, "I am not. Only God is." When we say man-God, God-man, the meaning is that when man is not there only God is, and when God is not there only man is. If the 'I' is not present, then God alone is present. But if God is not there, only the 'I' is present.

Only God can worship God. At this stage man does not exist. The 'I' does not exist. Thus there is no mind, desire, or intention. Everything within him has become the nature of God. At this time it is a current station, not a *māyā* station. If touched, only current will come forth. What exists now is a power station, not a station for mind or *māyā*. Anything that touches it will be burnt and flung far away. This is the stage of *illallāhu*.

---

7. *sūfi gnānam* (T) The fifth level of spiritual ascendance, beyond *sharī'at*, *tarīqat*, *haqīqat*, and *ma'rifat*; the state of one who has transcended the four religions and merged with God.

8. *salām* (s) (A) Greeting of peace.

salawāt (A) Praising and glorifying Allah and invoking peace upon the *Rasūl* ☽, the prophets, and the angels. The praise that you offer to Allah, the *Rasūl* ☽, and the heavenly beings comes back to you as your own treasure, your own wealth. The *salām* and *salawāt* you offer come back to you and light up your own face and heart. This is the reason that the *salām* and *salawāt* are considered to be very exalted.

The first stage, which is *lā ilāha*, pumps up the *karma* of this birth and pushes it out. The *lā ilāha* is carried on the breath, while the *illallāhu* is drawn along on the current. This must be experienced and understood. The *dhikr* should be done in the way I have explained. You need to get hold of that point and carry it to your feeling and awareness.

The correct way to do the *dhikr* is to draw it with your breath, in silent concentration, but when you are beginning, there is no harm if the words *lā ilāha, illallāhu* are spoken audibly. The movement of the *dhikr* should first be known within feeling and awareness. Intellect should be aware of which places it is passing through. When the movement of the *dhikr* touches the hair follicles and the nerves, they should feel it and vibrate, just as a violin string vibrates and produces music when it is plucked.

Bawa Muhaiyaddeen demonstrates.

This is how you should perform this *dhikr*. Sit properly, and start with *la-a-a-a* as you send the breath out through the left nostril. As the breath reaches the back of the tongue, the *la-a-a-a* continues as *laaa-il-laa-ha*. While awareness is carrying the *dhikr* along, divine analytic wisdom says, "*Lā ilāha*: Other than You there is nothing," and pushes the impure breath out. Feeling, awareness, and the other levels of consciousness should be aware of whether the sound has moved along.

The master musician will know it. When the nerves are being strummed by the *dhikr* and go *ting, ting, ting, ting* like the strings of the *vīna*, the One who is an expert in that music will recognize the melody, the rhythm, and the tune. That *Ūmaiyan* alone will know.

Question: Who is the *Ūmaiyan?*

Bawa Muhaiyaddeen: God. He is the silent One, the One who does not speak, the One who has studied this music. He alone will know the song, the thought, the intention, and the wisdom behind the strumming done in silence by the one doing the *dhikr*. Only that expert musician will be able to identify and distinguish those sounds—the beat, the melody, and what instrument it is. This is the music of prayer, and only that professor of music can understand it.

When the *dhikr* reaches the tip of the tongue, the 'flute' will send out the sound *la-a-a-a* which will resonate in all places. As the sound is separated by the flute, that musician will hear the *laaa-il-laa-ha*. The separating of that sound from the breath is effected by a fluttering of the eyelids, a flare of the nostrils, a twitching of the temples, and a quivering of the angles of the mouth—all on the left side, in the same way that a flutist moves his lips and makes facial movements in order to produce the fine tones of the musical notes.

As we then take the breath in on the right side, saying, "*Illallāhu,*" divine analytic wisdom, the sixth level of wisdom, makes contact with that which is wisdom within wisdom. At this time, the perception of the eye, of feeling, of awareness, of intellect, of subtle wisdom, and of divine analytic wisdom should all establish contact, while divine luminous wisdom checks to make sure they do. All the inner senses—the point within the eye, the point within the ear, the point within the nose, the point within the tongue, the point within feeling, the point within awareness—all of these should make contact with the place contacted by wisdom. Not this outer eye but the point within this eye must touch it, not this outer sense of smell but an inner one must go and touch it, not this ear but an inner ear, not this mouth but an inner mouth, not this heart but an inner heart (the *qalb*, where it must be installed) must go and touch it.

When all this has been done, when divine analytic wisdom (after separating and casting out all the unwanted things) has entered and touched that which is truth, that which is wisdom within wisdom, then feeling, awareness, intellect, and subtle wisdom should focus on it with concentration. While they all are observing carefully, divine analytic wisdom, looking intently at it and checking it, must pull it along, as if with pincers. All the others must be watching attentively.

As divine analytic wisdom checks that current out and draws it along to enter the right nostril, you must be perceiving the awareness that is monitoring it. Everything must be checked as this current goes along. From the nostril, it goes to the *kursī*, the eye of wisdom in the center of the forehead, halts there, and then spreads out through the brain, to reach the *'arsh*, at the crown of the head. From the *'arsh* it descends to the tongue, where it causes a vibration which brings forth the sound *illallāhu*. Then it goes beyond and is seated in the *qalb* as *hooo*, O God, You are Allah. You must bring forth this sound from that inner musical instrument and observe it with your awareness.

While divine luminous wisdom is checking the flow of this current, all the levels of consciousness must jointly be watching closely to see which cities, or stations, the current is flowing to from the *qalb*. This must be monitored by all the states of inner perception—the inner eye, the inner nose, the inner ear, the inner tongue, the inner *qalb*, the inner perception, inner awareness, inner intellect. All of these must closely monitor the flow of the current which is *illallāhu*. It is only when we look with this inner subtle perception that we will see the eighteen thousand universes within us. Our focus will now be in that realm.

This process may be compared to that of a king being conducted through his kingdom. All these forces that are concentratedly focused are like the king's commanders, vigilantly observing his every move along the route. They must not look here and there. They must focus on him alone. Similarly, as divine analytic wisdom conducts the king, God, from the *'arsh* to the *qalb*, all His guards (feeling, awareness, intellect, assessment, and subtle wisdom) are watching closely. Divine luminous wisdom is the supreme commander, maintaining overall supervision of the king's forces and His journey. All the while an inner eye should be looking, an inner ear listening, an inner tongue speaking, an inner nose smelling, and an inner *qalb* functioning. All these guards must constantly check where the king is going, the route, the area that He is traversing, how He is progressing, etc. A very close check must be maintained until He is conducted to His seat, the innermost heart, the *qalb*, saying, "*Illallāhu:* You are God!" Having installed the king in the innermost heart, the commander, the *Nūr*, turns on the switches in order to check all the stations to which the king must go—the nerves, blood vessels, muscles, and so on. This is the *dhikr*.

Thus when the current, or light, is settled in the innermost heart and the power is switched on, it will be distributed to all the fifteen worlds[9] instantly, as well as to the twelve stations or openings[10] in the body. The power that goes to two of these stations [the *'arsh* and the *kursī*] will reach the eighteen thousand universes within us. You should do the *dhikr* in this manner.

---

9. Bawa Muhaiyaddeen often spoke about the fifteen realms within the form of man. There are seven worlds above and seven worlds below. This world of the heart is in the center. This is the focal point for man. Explanations of this concept can be found in *The Guidebook to the True Secret of the Heart*, Vol. 2 pp.123-138 and in *The Wisdom of the Divine*, Vol. 3 p. 21, both by Bawa Muhaiyaddeen.

10. Bawa Muhaiyaddeen has explained that the twelve openings refers to two eyes, two ears, two nostrils, the mouth, the fecal opening, the sexual opening, the navel which has been cut and sealed, the *kursī* and the *'arsh*. The first ten are the planets that torment man. They are in the darkness of ignorance. When the light of *illallāhu* is established in the heart, it is distributed to all parts of the body, and these openings become filled with light.

Bawa Muhaiyaddeen demonstrates.

You must learn to concentrate pointedly while doing the *dhikr*. The *salām* of *illallāhu*, as well as the *lā ilāha*, should be done in the way I have described. The tip of the tongue should be able to isolate the breath and split it away.

⌁

This discourse should be checked and typed up and a copy given to every child in the Fellowship.[11] They should follow these points in their prayer. Let a copy be given to the children who are praying here [in Sri Lanka]. This is not for everyone. Send a copy to the Philadelphia Fellowship, and tell them this is how they should perform the *dhikr*. Those who are here should also follow this point by point. This is not a matter for public distribution. What I have just described is true prayer [*vanakkam*].

Questioner: We are keen to sit like you, to sit and do the prayer in the same way you do.

Bawa Muhaiyaddeen: You say so now, but putting it into practice is another matter.

Questioner: No, Bawangal! We do want to do it that way. We do not want to lose time.

Bawa Muhaiyaddeen: Then you must gather here at the right time. When I am awake and not doing anything in particular, if you gather around, I will instruct you and help you practice. You must sit as I do, you must breathe as I have described, and focus your attention one-pointedly. After you have practiced it in this way, then later you can do this prayer at any time, even while standing or walking. Once you have thrown out the unwanted portion and have trained awareness and divine analytic wisdom to establish contact with that which is wisdom within wisdom, with *illallāhu*, then divine analytic wisdom will continue it automatically. It is that simple. Until that happens you must practice.

However, you may find it difficult to control your mind and fix it on the desired point of focus. Therefore, only if you learn to concentrate all your forces with care, faith, and certitude will you succeed in performing

---

11. The central branch of the Bawa Muhaiyaddeen Fellowship is located in Philadelphia, Pennsylvania. The Fellowship serves as a meeting house and as a reservoir of people and materials for all who are interested in the teachings of M. R. Bawa Muhaiyaddeen. Branches of the Fellowship exist throughout the United States, and in Canada, England, and Sri Lanka.

this *dhikr* correctly. If, without focusing on the point, you allow your mind to stray here and there, then it will not be *dhikr*. Only if your focus and your senses come together at that one point will it be *dhikr*. When the king is setting out, all the commanders should be in attendance there and in control. That is how the *dhikr* must be done. All the levels of consciousness (feeling, awareness, intellect, assessment, subtle wisdom, divine analytic wisdom, and divine luminous wisdom) should be there.

The inner perception—not this sight but an inner seeing, not this hearing but an inner listening, not the senses that perceive the world but an inner nose, an inner tongue—all these should be checking on the *dhikr*. If you have attained this state, your physical eyes will not see. The inner eye will be seeing and perceiving an inner vision. The outer eye will be open but blocked from seeing, as though anesthetized. The nostrils will still inhale and exhale, but the sense of smell will be absent. There will be an inner sense of smell, drawing another fragrance, blocking out the odors of the world. The outer ears will still be there, but they will not hear the sounds of the world. They will be hearing another sound, from a different place. In the mouth, the tongue will be the same, but unable to speak, as if anesthetized. The inner tongue will be communing with another source. The heart and mind will function as before, but an inner *qalb* will be functioning at a different level.

Thus, in this state, the entire body stays as it was before. The eyes, the nose, the ears, the tongue are all there, but unaware of the world, anesthetized. Awareness is directed to an inner level, and so the senses cannot function in the world. Another level of awareness is now functioning. The sights and sounds and odors of the world are no longer perceived. The *qalb* is not in the world.

Such is the restraint with which this *dhikr* must be done. We have to subdue our senses and perceptions to this extent, in order to do this *dhikr*. This is the true prayer, wherein all the king's commanders stand at one point, not scattered around and functioning in the world.

This is the way you must perform *dhikr*. This alone is true worship. If faith, certitude, and determination are functioning steadily, the external senses will be anesthetized. If you have reached the correct point of concentration, your ears will not hear any outer sounds. If you begin to do the *dhikr* correctly, those ears will not hear. The outer eyes will have lost the power to see what is there. The sense of smell which perceives the odors of this world will be absent. The tongue will have lost the power to respond to the speech of the world. The mind, the heart, which runs after the desires and attachments of the world will not function here. Only God will be in command. The only speech at that time will be the direct communion between wisdom and God. All the other sections, although not dead, will cease to function. They will be closed off, anesthetized.

This prayer, done in this state of inner focus, is true prayer. It is the original prayer. What I am describing is not a prayer done through the senses or with the mind. It is not a prayer done by earth, fire, water, air, or ether. It cannot be done through magic or mantras. It is not the kind performed by the various religions. It cannot be done with racial bigotry, caste, discriminations, or dogmas. This prayer can be performed only with the point of *īmān*, the firm faith, certitude, and determination that there is nothing but God. It is a prayer performed as wisdom within wisdom. It is the *dhikr* in which wisdom searches for and finds that thing which is wisdom within wisdom, the prayer which discovers the One to whom *awwal*, *dunyā*, and *ākhirah*[12] belong, the prayer in which we find God through God.

It is a prayer in which:

> God is realized through His truth,
> God is realized through His qualities,
> God is realized through His actions,
> God is realized through His patience,
> God is realized through His contentment [*shakūr*],
> God is realized through His inner patience [*sabūr*],
> God is realized through His *tawakkul* [giving all responsibility
>   to God],
> God is realized through surrender to Him,
> God is realized through His word [*kalimah*],
> God is known through His speech,
> God is realized through His innermost heart [*qalb*],
> God is worshiped in the temple that He built,
> He is realized through His own name and His word,
>   "There is nothing else. Other than Me there is no God,"

---

12. *awwal*, *dunyā*, and *ākhirah* (A) The beginning, this world, and the hereafter.

> God is realized by the essence of purity of the light called *dīn*,
> God is realized by the light called *is-lām*,
>> We discard desires [*'ishq*] and realize Him by the light
>> called *lām*,
> God is realized through His revelations [*wahys*],
> God is realized through His sound,
> God is seen through His sight,
> God's fragrance is realized by His own fragrance,
> God is realized by speaking to Him with His own tongue,
>> the tongue of *īmān*.
> We commune with Him through His own heart [*qalb*].

This is *dhikr*. This is the *dhikr* I have been talking about. Unless you have this conduct and have reached this state, the *dhikr* cannot be done properly. This *dhikr*, *lā ilāha, illallāhu*, is the original point. It was God's word in *anāthi* before *āthi*.[13] It was the word that emerged even before creation. This is the word that emanated from within Him prior to the creation, four *yugas* [two hundred million years] ago, given as divine instruction to the light that emanated from Him. It is the word that was revealed in the time before creation, when God existed alone, as Himself. This was the word given as instruction to His representative, the *Nūr*, the complete, perfect light that came from within Him. This word resonated as the explanation at a time when lives were just being manifested as the lights of atoms, before they were given form. This was the word given before *awwal* [the beginning]. It was the atoms that manifested from this word that became the creations. The magnetic and electrical currents that issued as sparks from this word became the six kinds of lives.

When you initially analyze those six kinds of lives, five of them will be seen as earth lives, water lives, fire lives, air lives, and ether lives (color or light lives such as the sun and the moon). The sixth life, the human soul, is God's ray, a resplendent ray from His light, the *Nūr*. The human life is the power of God. It is a complete power. It is perfect. This life, the human soul, is endowed with the seven levels of wisdom: feeling, awareness, intellect, assessment, subtle wisdom, divine analytic wisdom, and

---

13. *anāthi* before *āthi* (T) *Āthi* is the time when the light of the *Nūr* and the wisdom of the *Qutbiyyat* manifested within Allah. *Anāthi* is the beginningless beginning, the time before *āthi*, when nothing had been manifested, and Allah was by Himself.

divine luminous wisdom. This is the life known as Adam.

When you who have this life, which is from the light of perfection [the *Nūr*], come to examine with the light of that wisdom the six kinds of life, you will see that they are really: feeling-life, awareness-life, intellect-life, assessment-life, subtle wisdom-life, and divine analytic wisdom-life. When that sixth life, the divine analytic wisdom-life (the perfect, complete life that came from the *Nūr)* moves inward to touch that which is wisdom within wisdom, the other five kinds of life should also be assembled there, as commanders. Divine luminous wisdom, the commander-in-chief, which is the light of perfection, the light of the *Nūr,* monitors this. Only when all six, standing as one, focus on and continue to check the *dhikr* will it be the true *dhikr.*

This *dhikr* does not belong within the religions. It is possible only in the state that transcends caste and religious differences. It occurs only beyond scriptures and religious texts. This is the prayer of *ma'rifat,* the state of prayer that has neither day nor night, only light. There is no sleep or awakening, nothing is lacking, and there is no destruction. Prayer in this station of fullness and perfection is known as *ma'rifat.*[14]

It is the prayer of *sūfiyyat,*[15] in which you, as God, see God. Here you transcend everything and are in the kingdom of God. This is prayer performed in the kingdom of God, in the *'arsh,* the throne of God, where you pray along with Him. It is not a prayer of this world. It is a prayer that is prayed in heaven [*ākhirah*]. It is a prayer performed in His presence, when one is face to face with Him. This you must understand.

If all the commanders are not focused at that one place, if even one strays away into religion, or race, or scriptures, or philosophy, if all are not joined in one place, this prayer will not turn out right. If your senses are not anesthetized, it is not this prayer. If your outer eyes are seeing, if you are hearing the sounds from the world, it is not this prayer. If you are experiencing the smells of the world, it is not this prayer. If you are talking, it is not this prayer. If your heart is looking at the world, it is not this prayer.

---

14. *ma'rifat* (A) Gnosis, the fourth level of spiritual ascendancy, beyond *sharī'at, tarīqat,* and *haqīqat;* a state of union with God.

15. *sūfiyyat* (A) The fifth level of spiritual ascendancy, beyond *sharī'at, tarīqat, haqīqat,* and *ma'rifat;* the state of one who has transcended the four religions, transformed himself into the state of God, and merged with God.

Just as a patient in surgery under general anesthesia retains his awareness of being cut open but feels no pain and cannot speak, so must you anesthetize your senses and retain awareness only of Him. You must speak only with Him. This is the prayer of *dhikr*.

This prayer will not be taught in any of the religions or found in any scriptures. It is the word of God, spoken by God to His completeness. Establish this state with certitude. Pray in this way, and within this awareness you will see the eighteen thousand universes. Through this awareness alone can you commune with your *guru*. He is right there within wisdom. Because of this, if you contact that wisdom with this awareness, and then ask your questions, he will answer you. If you ask him where heaven is, he will show you. The answer will come as a vibration. At this time, all speech will be his, not yours. The focus will be yours, the wisdom will be yours, but the speech will be his. Your only function will be to direct your focus and intention totally on him, while you ask the questions of him. They will not be asked in the usual way. They will be asked by your feeling, by your awareness, by your intellect, by your assessment, and by your subtle wisdom.

When all of these are assembled around your *guru*, which is divine analytic wisdom [*qutbiyyat*], that *guru* will speak. But you must touch with your feeling, ask with your awareness and intellect, control with your assessment, and understand with subtle wisdom. Then the *guru* will speak. It will come as a vibration. It will not be you speaking. You should not ask with the tongue, or with the eyes, or with the nose, or with the mouth. You will be asking from an inner realm. When you ask from your awareness, he will speak from within. Your awareness and feeling will know it. Your intellect will know it. It will be shown. It will also come as a vibration. Assessment will know where each thing is. Subtle wisdom will identify each thing, saying, "Aha, this is the heavenly world, this is the world of hell, this is the world of sin, this is the world of *māyā*," and so on. Not only will it be heard within as words, it will also be seen as scenes. The *rūh*, or life, will be perceived by wisdom. Everything will be visible. You will perceive heaven, you will perceive hell, you will perceive God, you will see the angels, the archangels, and the prophets. You will be seeing and hearing all of these with your wisdom and your awareness.

If you have installed that *guru* which is divine analytic wisdom within you, then your only duty will be to observe through that. That *guru* will summon your feeling and awareness and the others, saying, "Come along," and fly around, carrying you. You will see everything, as if you were watching a television screen. As you go on asking, the answers will be shown, as if on a screen. If a thought arises in your awareness or your wisdom, the moment the question comes to your intellect, a direct answer will come as a vibration. It will be a direct explanation, given face to face, a direct vision, seen as if on television. The moment you ask, you will instantly be able to perceive the eighteen thousand universes.

It is in this way that you must speak to him, through feeling, awareness, intellect, assessment, subtle wisdom, and divine analytic wisdom. These are matters that can be understood only at the level of wisdom, matters relating to the manifested universe [*'ālam*], the unseen, or invisible, divine realm [*arwāh*], and all of everything. When you ask something in this state of awareness, it is another who is listening, and the answer will come in the form of a vibration. It is not you who will be speaking. The words will be coming from him. When you reach this state, you will be like a microphone. The sound will rise up within you, and the microphone, which is you, will transmit it to the outside, where it will be heard by others.

Once you attain this state, these eyes will be transformed. The pores on your skin, the hair, bones, muscles, and eyes will transform into light. After this, your eyes may be looking here and there, but they will see only God in everything they perceive. Only His wonders will be seen. Only His speech will be heard. You will see nothing of the world. The only thing you will see is Him. Your whole body will be transformed into the form of light. The dark section of illusion [*māyā*] will have disappeared.

Now, as soon as awareness asks to see something, it will be shown at once. If it requests, "Show the *'arsh*," it will be shown. If it asks, "What is the destiny of this person?" that will be shown. "What is the good and evil in this person?" that will be seen. "What do the angels do?" All these will be revealed. If it requests, "Show me *awwal*," the beginning of creation will unfold. Everything will be seen right where you are. Such is the bliss this prayer brings. You must do this with understanding.

This is not just something you talk about. You must really work on it. You must be the commander, going ahead of the king, commanding the six kinds of lives: earth lives, fire lives, water lives, air lives, ether lives, and soul lives. Once these come into contact with the power of God (the light which is the *Nūr*, that soul which is human life), they must transform into the six levels of wisdom: feeling, awareness, intellect, assessment, subtle wisdom, and divine analytic wisdom. Divine analytic wisdom is the form of the *guru*, the *guru*-life, the *qutbiyyat*. *Qutbiyyat* is the life that came from the *Nūr*. That is the *sayyid*,[16] the *shaikh*, Faqīr Muhaiyaddeen Mujāhidatullāh ☺[17] It is the *shaikh*, the *qutbiyyat*, initiating you as disciples. It is giving you grace. It is giving you wisdom. It is giving you light. It gives you understanding, and embraces you. This is the *Qutb*.

Try to understand this and resolve to attain this state. Perform the *dhikr* in this way, from today on. This is the prayer [*vanakkam*] practiced by this *shaikh*, your *shaikh*. In this prayer, with God's gaze, you perform 43,242 prostrations to God each day. That is, God worships Himself. Since you are prostrating to Him with every breath, this prayer goes on at every second, whether you are walking or sitting, sleeping or awake. This is the point. Do you understand? This is the way it must be done.

This is the word your *shaikh*, the *qutbiyyat*, spoke to the Perfection in *arwāh* [the invisible divine realm]. This is the prayer in *arwāh*, the prayer in which God is worshiped directly by the state of God. It is not easy. It is not a prayer that the world will do. Only one group among human beings, a very rare group, will do this. You must all join that group in which each one, as God, worships God. Only one group out of the seventy-three groups of people has been granted this power. You must become that power. You must join that power, that one group. The other seventy-two groups are destined for hell. They will not understand this prayer. Therefore, you must understand and develop this *dhikr* within you. This is true prayer.

[The *shaikh* says,] "My children! *As-salāmu 'alaikum*. I am one of perfect purity."

We should respond with, "'*Alaikumus-salām*. We too are of perfect purity."

God says, "*As-salāmu 'alaikum*. I am perfect purity. I am Islam."

---

16. *sayyid* (A) A master.

17. Faqīr Muhaiyaddeen Mujāhidatullāh ☺: The name of the *Qutb* of this age.
   Faqīr: A poor mendicant.
   Muhaiyaddeen: Reviver of the *dīn*, the path of perfect purity.
   Mujāhidatullāh: One who has steadfast determination on the path to Allah.

We say, *"'Alaikumus-salām.* I am also of perfect purity. I too worship You. I belong to the same family, man-God, God-man."

"As-salāmu 'alaikum." We must offer these *salāms* to Him, and He will reciprocate. *"'Alaikumus-salām.* I am that too." Both should be in the same state.

April 21, 1974

CHAPTER THREE

Questions and Answers

Question: What is the explanation of the Tamil word *niyyatthu?*

Bawa Muhaiyaddeen: *Niyyatthu* is the intention for God. It is the focus on God in every duty one undertakes.

Question: Is it similar to faith, certitude, and determination?

Bawa Muhaiyaddeen: There is a slight difference in each of these. Faith is one thing, certitude is a point within that, and determination is a point even deeper within that. *Niyyatthu* is a different word, not related to these three.

Question: You mentioned blowing on a flute when we say, "*Lā ilāha.*"

Bawa Muhaiyaddeen: I used that as an example. When one strums a *vīna* [an Indian stringed instrument] or blows into a flute, a sound comes forth. Only the flutist will know the sound he wants to make. The movements made by the tongue determine the musical notes emitted. Similarly, as the breath of the *dhikr* flows along saying, "*Lā ilāha:* There is nothing other than You," the movements of the tip of the tongue separate the sound from the breath. Who will recognize the musical sound that is emitted? God will. He is the only One who understands this music. Others will not understand it. Just as only the flutist knows what sounds he intends, this prayer will be recognized only by God.

Question: You said that when we say, "*Illallāhu,*" divine analytic wisdom should contact the treasure that is wisdom within wisdom.

Bawa Muhaiyaddeen: Yes. As you say, "*Lā ilāha,*" divine analytic wisdom should separate and discard the wrong. Then saying, "*Illallāhu:* Only You are God," it should carry the *hū* of *illallāhu* to divine luminous wisdom and then carry the point to the innermost heart [*qalb*] and install the truth there.

Question: When we say God exists as wisdom within wisdom, does He exist within the fifth level of wisdom?

Bawa Muhaiyaddeen: The fifth level is the wisdom of the senses. As the breath goes out, the sixth level of wisdom, saying, "*Lā ilāha,*" separates all that is wrong and pushes it out then takes the truth, the *illallāhu,* and installs it in the *qalb.*

Question: So, since God is the wisdom within wisdom, isn't it wisdom that makes the connection and draws God along? That is, isn't it divine analytic wisdom, the sixth level, that has to make that connection?

Bawa Muhaiyaddeen: That is correct. Divine analytic wisdom must merge into divine luminous wisdom.

Once the *dhikr* has been split off by divine analytic wisdom and the wrong has been discarded, divine analytic wisdom will point to God, then draw Him along and install Him in the *qalb* saying, "*Illallāhu:* Only You are God." Once the wrong has been discarded with the *lā ilāha,* divine analytic wisdom drags the *illallāhu* from that point to the right nostril.

Question: What is that point?

Bawa Muhaiyaddeen: That point is Allah, truth. Divine analytic wisdom focuses on a point which represents Allah, and draws it, saying, "*Illallāhu.*" That is, the sixth level of wisdom attaches itself to the light, the *Nūr,* and to God.

Thus divine analytic wisdom, having done the separating, points to the light of the *Nūr* and draws it along. It is within divine luminous wisdom [*Nūr*] that God exists. So two points are drawn along (divine luminous wisdom and God) and installed, saying, "*Illallāhu.*" The eyes flutter when this happens, indicating that something is leaving and that wisdom is pointing and drawing something along. The movement of the eye is the point that draws the breath along.

Question: Isn't the trembling of the eye merely a physical phenomenon, related to the body?

Bawa Muhaiyaddeen: It is not a physical phenomenon. The movement actually draws the *dhikr* along. It has to do with the separating, but neither is it a voluntary movement like winking. It indicates an awareness.

Bawa Muhaiyaddeen demonstrates.

When that movement occurs, it means that it is separating something and drawing it along.

Question: When we say, "*Illallāhu,*" it should all be God, shouldn't it? There should be nothing to separate.

Bawa Muhaiyaddeen: The breath has to be taken over to the right side. It is through the movement of the eye that the switching of the flow of the breath is recognized. It is rather like understanding something by seeing a negative of it. Without it, you will not understand where the breath is flowing. Until you reach a certain stage, you need to be aware of where the breath is coming and going. After that it will become automatic and the facial movements will cease to be necessary. It will flow as automatically as the life or soul [*rūh*] flows through us. It will function as traffic lights do, with one light stopping cars and the other telling them to go. Just as the green and red lights keep flashing, it too will function automatically, but it will not operate like that until later. For now it needs to be like this. This is the stage of learning.

Question: When we translated what you said earlier, we wrote, "Divine analytic wisdom goes and contacts the One within wisdom." It appears as though divine analytic wisdom, which is the sixth level, contacts the One within the fifth level.

Bawa Muhaiyaddeen: That sixth level should fall into the seventh level of wisdom and drag it from there.

Question: Bawangal, you said that when we are in the state of *dhikr*, it is as though our eyes and ears are anesthetized. Even if the eyes are open they see nothing. You also said that the mind continues to run about as before.

Bawa Muhaiyaddeen: That is not correct. The mind cannot be running about. It must come to a halt at this stage. It is only when the mind has been stilled that the *dhikr* can be performed properly.

Question: Bawangal, you have said that at this stage our *guru* will be within us and whatever question we ask, it will be the *guru* who answers us.

Bawa Muhaiyaddeen: Yes, if you have attained this state, that is what will happen. But that takes a long time.

Question: You have said that at this stage we will be like a microphone.

Bawa Muhaiyaddeen: Yes, that is how it will be. If you have placed the *guru* within you, then as soon as you think of a question, he will answer within a second. Everything he has taught you, all the answers he has given to your questions, will be within you. When you ask a question about something you do not understand, such as, "I wish to see heaven," it should be wisdom that does the asking. Only the sixth level of wisdom [divine analytic wisdom] can separate or discriminate in this way. It has to transcend and stand beyond the five levels of wisdom, which relate to the senses. Having done this, it must ask God, who is the treasure that is within the seventh level of wisdom [divine luminous wisdom].

Then, when it asks the question, the answer will come forth as a vibration. Not only will the answer come forth, it will be known both within the body and on the outside. The answer will be known even when the eyes are closed. It will be known in every section of the body. The path will be seen, the answer will be known, and the manner in which it comes and goes will be known. It will be similar to viewing things through a microscope. Everything can be seen within the innermost heart [*qalb*].

Question: The answer will be heard within, but…

Bawa Muhaiyaddeen: Divine analytic wisdom will hear it.

Question: But only if we then say the answer out loud will others hear it.

Bawa Muhaiyaddeen: You can reveal it to others. The vibration that comes can be recorded within you. When it enters, it will be stored in the 'reserve' brain, at the back of the head. Later, when you try to tell it to someone, that which has been stored in the 'reserve' place will flow into divine analytic wisdom and can then be repeated to others.

Question: Bawangal, do we say this deliberately or does it emerge on its own?

Bawa Muhaiyaddeen: It is not 'you' who speaks. Everything you said to the *guru* and heard from him is stored in the reserve brain, at the back of the head. The answers you seek and attain on the inside are stored there. These are what you now repeat. Whatever you try to say on your own is useless. If the 'I' exists—if you think that it is you who is speaking—the answers will not come. But if the 'I' is not functioning, the answers will keep coming.

Question: Bawangal, you said that it is only when the physical senses are anesthetized that this can be understood on the inside. Therefore, is it possible to speak on the outside at the same time that we hear the answer on the inside?

Bawa Muhaiyaddeen: No, it is not possible. The vibration will be speaking to the vibration. At that time you cannot speak. At that stage of prayer you cannot speak. You will be comprehending what you are hearing within and will not be aware of anything else. The way you comprehend it will be such that you cannot convey it to others.

If, after having stored all of this, you wish to reveal it to others, then you must first say, "I am not." For example, when you need to reply to a question you should say, "Not I, but my *guru* must please speak!" Say this, think it, and then start speaking. The answer will come forth. If you keep looking at your heart for a little while, the answer will be seen at once. You will see your *guru* right away. Even if, instead of looking at your heart you look upward, you will see your *guru* there. You will hear his speech. But, if you think, "*I* am going to say something," what you say will not be right.

Even if it is the Angel of Death, 'Izrā'īl ☺, who comes to ask the questions, the right answers will be forthcoming. It does not matter who asks the question, the answer will be given. It does not matter what question is asked, the answer will be such that it makes any further questions unnecessary. No matter how many openings there are for further questions, the answer will satisfy all of them. It will be such that others will accept it and stop asking.

Question: Bawangal has told us that when we say, "*Illallāhu,*" the *dhikr* is meant to carry the power of God from the *'arsh* down to the heart, and that power is then utilized to light up the whole body and all the universes within us. But why do we have to draw it down to the heart [*qalb*]? Why don't we tap the power directly from the *'arsh* and use it to light up the body?

Bawa Muhaiyaddeen: God is everywhere, is He not? Now, to dig a well, one first needs to dig in a place from which the water can gush forth. It is not possible to reach the water at ground level, from the top of the well. One must dig deep down and open up the eye of the spring. Only then will water seep into the well, and only then can it be drawn up to be distributed in every direction, to all the fields. We cannot tap the water from the top, can we? The well has to be dug deep and the spring opened.

The openings to the springs are in the heart. [Bawa Muhaiyaddeen points to the crown of the head]. This is the *'arsh.* It is the throne where God sits. It is the place of judgment. The innermost heart [*qalb*] is the place of prayer, the *'arshul-mu'min,* the station of God, the house of God. So where should one be—at the court of justice or in the place of prayer? If, of course, you have attained the position of supreme judge, then you can sit in the court. But for now the place of prayer is in the *qalb*, for both king and pauper.

Even though the world is vast, it can be summarized in two words—*isn't* and *is*. Similarly, no matter how much is written, it can all be revealed in two words. And even though God exists everywhere, within everything, it all can be summarized in these two words—*isn't* and *is*.

There are two paths: the path that sends to the east what needs to go to the east, and the path that sends to the west what needs to go to the west. It is like two train tracks. For example, in Sri Lanka, from the Polgahawela railway junction people can travel in four different directions. The tracks can take them to Badulla, Colombo, Jaffna, or Nuwara Eliya. From Polgahawela two lines go toward the east and one toward the west. The *'arsh* is like this junction, a meeting place where things get sorted out and sent to the four different religions. Those that came from the east and want to go straight through to the west are given what they need and allowed to proceed saying, "*Illallāhu.*" Those that want to go back to the east are helped to change trains so they can return to the east. *Lā ilāha* is used to re-route things to the east, and *illallāhu* is used to send things on to the west. Thus the whole matter can be contained in these two words.

After you practice this for a while, it will come out right. Say it aloud, then say it silently. Say it with awareness, say it with wisdom, say it with feeling, say it with intellect, say it with judgment, say it with the fifth level, and then say it after you have analyzed and separated it with divine analytic wisdom. As you continue to practice, it will begin to work correctly on its own. Proceed slowly, and it will come out right in the end.

Trying to tap the energy from the top, from the *'arsh*, is of no use. God can be worshiped only in His church. One has to proceed slowly.

We have given a very good explanation about silence, about the *dhikr* of the heart and the *dhikr* of the soul. This can be done in silence, with no outer sound. The inner sound goes on within. You should study that explanation. It is very subtle.

May 18, 1974

Question: When we want to do *dhikr*, in the morning or evening, we want to sit in a certain position, in order to get an intensity of experience that would not be there otherwise.

Bawa Muhaiyaddeen: That is the way people usually think about it. It is sort of like someone who is getting totally soaked by a heavy rain thinking he must take a bath. He fails to realize the rain is giving him a good bath. He is getting fully soaked by it, yet he believes that only if he gets into the tub or shower will he really bathe. This is just a thought his mind brings to him. In the same way, your mind makes you think you have to go to a certain place and sit in a particular position in order to do *dhikr*. But if you do the *dhikr* as you walk along and understand that you are getting soaked in it—provided you have that intention and determination—you will derive the same benefit, the same grace, as from sitting in the customary place and position. In spite of all the noise and all the distractions in the world, if you have that intention in you, then you will be doing the *dhikr* wherever you may be.

Question: Bawa Muhaiyaddeen has told us earlier that in order to get that intention fixed firmly, before beginning the *dhikr* proper, we must first recite the *Subhānallāhi Kalimah* and some *sūrats* from the *Qur'ān*.

Bawa Muhaiyaddeen: The *Subhānallāhi Kalimah* is a light for the dark house of our inner heart [*qalb*]. We recite it in order to cut away all that is there and to attach a light to each of the wires. We recite it to install the light that will clear this house before beginning prayer.

To come to this state, we first must sacrifice all the animals in the inner heart [*qalb*], slaughter all the monkeys there. That is, we offer the *qalb* itself in sacrifice. In so doing, we make that inner heart perfectly pure [*halāl*] and then install the light there. Having done this, we glorify Allah. Only after the inner heart has been cleared out and made pure can one glorify Allah. This is the reason for the *Subhānallāhi Kalimah*.

A large number of prophets have recited this *kalimah*, even the *Hayāt Nabī*.[1] Qutb Muhaiyaddeen ☺ has recited it. Prophets and illumined beings have recited it. Thus it is good for our *qalbs* too if we recite it. First recite the Third *Kalimah*, then glorify Allah.

Question: Should we recite the *kalimah* and the *sūrats* every single time before we start doing the *dhikr*?

Bawa Muhaiyaddeen: If the light has developed in your *qalb* and does

---

1. *Hayāt Nabī:* The Eternal Prophet; the Prophet of life existing eternally as the sixth level of consciousness, divine analytic wisdom.

not go out, then you need not repeat it each time. Once the lamp is lit, there is no need to turn the switch on again. It is already clear within. But if the house is dark, you must flick the switch every time in order to turn on the light. As long as the world and the desires [*nafs*] remain in your heart you need to recite this. If there are no desires and no world, it is not necessary, for light is already there. Until then, it is advisable to do it.

Question: What is the meaning of having the *dhikr* on the breath? What is the difference between that and having the words going on in the mind? I am confused about having the *dhikr* on my breath and the words in my mind.

Bawa Muhaiyaddeen: Suppose you are sitting comfortably and an itch suddenly develops on your foot. You would be aware of it, would you not? Or if a mosquito bites you, you would know, would you not? And you would know exactly where the feeling is, where it hurts or itches. Then, why should you not be aware of the *dhikr?* You should be aware of the feeling caused by the movement of the *dhikr,* where it is in the body now, and the way it is moving up and down. It is wisdom, not the desires, that must know where and when that current, that power, rises up, stops, and moves on. Just as a voltage tester can detect the flow of current in a wire, wisdom must check, in a most subtle manner, the flow of the *dhikr.*

December 23, 1976

Question: Where is the point of the *Nūr?* Is it in the *'arsh?*

Bawa Muhaiyaddeen: It is everywhere. How can I show it to you? How can it be described? It is everywhere, but in order to give it a location, we say it is at the *'arsh.*

Question: When we breathe in saying, "*Illallāhu,*" what is the point from which the breath should be drawn?

Bawa Muhaiyaddeen: The innermost heart [*qalb*] must connect with the power that is Allah, with the light that is that power. You must have the certitude that Allah is a power without limit, without beginning or end, without equal or partner. Your certitude [*īmān*], and your intention and focus must go and connect with that power. When you look at that point of connection, you must perceive the light. The intensity of your focus should recognize this light, and the breath of the *dhikr* must focus on and be directed to that point. Your focus, the focus of your vision, must fall into it. The *dhikr* must go and fall into that point. It goes up saying, *"Lā ilāha,"* and is exhaled on the left side, saying, "There is nothing other than You." That is the point that must be focused upon. The breath which says, "There is nothing other than You," goes out, and your intention moves along with it.

Your next breath must be drawn from that power, that point, which is *illallāh:* You are Allah. Your intention, your focus, your strong determination, and the breath, the *dhikr,* must all move along, touch that power, grasp it with that intention, and pull it along. Once it is drawn from there, it must be firmly established, saying, *"Illallāh:* You are Allah." Then it will spread all over. You may think you are storing it in the one place, but the current will run to all places. All the nerves and blood vessels will know it and feel it. All the nerves, the hair follicles, the skin pores, and blood cells will experience it moving along. That is the correct way to do the *dhikr.*

Question: So the eye should be focused outside?

Bawa Muhaiyaddeen: It does not matter whether it is focused outside or in the inner heart [*qalb*], or whether the eyes are open or closed. What matters is that that point must merge and dwell in Him. You must take form within your yearning [*niyyat*]. You must become the point that is He.

Question: When you say, *"Lā ilāha,"* is it only expelling?

Bawa Muhaiyaddeen: You are saying, "Except for You there is nothing else. Go away. I am not. Only You are, O God."

Question: Is this a *dhikr* or a *kalimah?*

Bawa Muhaiyaddeen: It could be many things. For instance, when one speaks of the eyes, he may be referring to the light in the eyes, or the eyelids or eyebrows, or the tiny black pupil, or the white of the eye. All of these relate to the eye, but the thing that really matters is the light in the eye.

Similarly, it is *kalimah*, it is *dhikr*, it is prayer, it is wisdom, and it is a resonance. There are so many ways to perceive it, because its power varies according to how much it is sifted and separated. That power is utilized according to the needs of the place that uses it. For example, when a current goes to a motor, it burns up gasoline. If it goes to a light bulb, it gives light. If it goes to a welding machine, it welds. If it goes to a cutting place, it cuts. If it goes to a mixing machine, it mixes things together. If a fan has to rotate, it makes it rotate. It can record a word. It can amplify a sound or reduce it, to provide silence. The same current can be used in a variety of ways, and in each case it may be called by a different name.

Question: During *dhikr,* when I say, *"Lā ilāha,"* when I am cleansing the impurities and animal qualities from myself, where do they go? Do I give them to God, or do they just...

Bawa Muhaiyaddeen: *Lā ilāha* means: There is nothing other than You, O God! Whatever has to go to the world of hell will go to hell.

If you strike on gold you will produce the sound gold makes. If you strike iron you will produce the sound of iron. If you strike mud you will hear only the dull thump of mud.

Similarly, if the words of your prayer and meditation are like gold, the sound of gold will come back to you. The sound of God's voice, the sound of His power, will come forth. You will receive a reply appropriate to the sound you make. If, however, you are like iron, the noise made by your body and the mind of the five elements will be the noise of iron. And if you use the sound of your desires [*nafs*], the sound that comes back to you will be like the dull thump of mud.

This is the way it works. The response you receive to your *dhikr* depends on how and in what state you use it.

CHAPTER FOUR

The Prayer of a Sufi

In February 1978, Johannes Witteween was visiting Sri Lanka in his official capacity as Managing Director of The International Monetary Fund. Eager to meet a Sufi teacher, he expressed his interest to the people he was with, and they brought him to meet Bawa Muhaiyaddeen. After speaking with him that evening, Mr. Witteween expressed a wish to meditate along with him and was asked to return at 4:30 the following morning. It was then that Bawa Muhaiyaddeen gave the following discourse about the dhikr: lā ilāha, illallāhu, *as performed by Sufis.*

*M*y brother, there is something I would like to tell you about. We have gathered together here for early morning prayer. It is customary for people of all religions to gather in this way for prayer. In Islam they gather five prescribed times each day. In some religions they pray three times a day, in some twice, and in others just once a day. But no one has ever seen God. There is no one who has seen God with his eyes. However, man has an awareness of a certain mystery within. That feeling demonstrates and proves to him that there is 'something' within that carries him and keeps him going when he feels he just cannot go on. Although he is able to accomplish many things by himself, there are times when a man feels helpless. At such times, that something is there doing what is needed, thus demonstrating to his awareness and his wisdom the existence of something beyond. Man calls that something God.

This thing called God cannot be seen as a sun, a moon, a star, or any form. It is useless to try to imagine what it is like by comparing it with things that can be seen. Therefore, man wonders what God looks like. He makes statues of various animals (dogs, cats, elephants, peacocks, vultures, eagles) and wonders if God could be like any of them. He believes in them and worships them as gods.

Thus different groups try to formulate some image for God, based upon their degree of faith and their level of wisdom and intellect. But no matter what they create or how they worship, they all share the belief, the inner awareness, the mysterious feeling, that there is something far,

far beyond what they can see or imagine. This something within not only provides man with explanations and enables him to do things that are beyond him, it also builds his faith in the existence of God. Such faith does exist within each of us, telling us that there is a mystery working within us, a mystery we cannot understand.

The word 'secret' implies that an answer can be found. A mystery, however, is something that eludes us, even when we think we have grasped it. It remains beyond our knowing. We call this mystery, this power, God. Some deny that there is such a power. Others make idols and worship them as gods. Some even worship animal forms as gods. Still others say, "Yes, there is a power, but it is not a form, it is a light." This is how it is. Many, many methods of worship like this are practiced. Those who follow these practices believe in them as true forms of prayer.

Truth, however, lies in an altogether different domain. True prayer is not at all like any of the prayers we have seen. To do this prayer, the one who is praying and the One who is being prayed to must be one. They have to be one. That is true prayer. It is very, very hard to find anyone in the world who actually practices this true form of prayer. Such beings are extremely rare.

Different people pray in different ways. Different religions and scriptures teach different prayers. Islam prescribes five times of prayer [*waqts*] a day. Let us talk a little about this. In Islam, people turn from the east to the west and pray facing the direction of the *qiblah*.[1] They say that by worshiping in this manner, they are facing Allah and praying to Him. However, according to the understanding of the Sufis, God exists everywhere, in every place, in every direction. There is no place where God is not. There is no place where God cannot be known, for He exists within everything as a power. Just as water exists within the earth and air exists everywhere, just as fragrance exists within a flower and heat exists within earth and rocks, so a light, an essence, exists within each created thing. This power of God exists within all lives, all creations, making them grow. God is within everything. There is no place where He is not. This is what Sufis realize.

Islam says that when you pray you must face toward the west, toward

---

1. *qiblah:* The direction Muslims face when they pray, turning toward the *Ka'bah*, in Mecca. For people who live in the east (as in Sri Lanka), Mecca is westward.

the *qiblah*, but to a Sufi, the whole world is a prayer mat. Wherever he may be, in whatever direction he may turn, he can pray to God. There- fore, what is the real meaning regarding east and west? The 'east' signifies man's creation, his birth, his appearing. And what is the 'west'? That is where he comes to his end. That is his disappearing. He appears in the east and disappears in the west. When Islam says, "Face toward the west," it really means that man must disappear in prayer. He was born in the east, and now he must die in the west, die in his prayer. He must lose the self. The west is the final state, in which he loses himself in God.

Thus, a Sufi speaks of the east as the place where all man's thoughts appear, while the west is the place where all that appeared will disappear and die. His thoughts, his mind, his desires, his form—all these will be subdued, condensed, brought under control, and made to die. Prayer, for him, is to lose himself, to die in God, in total surrender to Him. This is true prayer. If he wants to reach God, whatever worlds he holds within himself must leave him. They must die. Only if his self dies can this hap- pen. The world in which he appeared must be made to separate from him and disappear. Only then can he see the station he was in before he ar- rived. Where was he earlier? What state was he in then? From what place did he come? He was in God before he came to this world, and only if the world dies from him can he go back to that which he came from, to God.

No matter who it is that is praying, if, when he prays, his self has died, then it can be said that he has truly prayed. That is prayer. For a Sufi, the only true prayer is the prayer done in this state. Only when one attains this state and prays in this way can it be called true prayer.

The prayer of a Sufi does not require being seated in a particular man- ner or posture. This is not necessary. What is required of a Sufi? Every one of the 43,242 breaths taken every twenty-four hours must connect with God. Only when his every breath connects with God, constantly interacting with Him, can one be known as a Sufi. This means speaking without talking, smiling without smiling, seeing without looking, under- standing without thinking, walking without walking, sleeping without sleeping, and eating without eating. There are many such subtle mean- ings within what we call Sufism.

For a Sufi, prayer consists of prostrating [*sajdah*] to God 43,242 times each day, because with every breath he lays his forehead at the feet of God. Each breath draws him into the state of surrender to God. This prayer cannot be fulfilled by praying three or five times a day. Sufism is not a state of exhilaration and delusion like that derived from taking marijuana and opium. Sufism is not getting married and raising children. Sufism, or *Sūfi-sun*, means to be a *sun* to the world, and *Sūfi-son* means to be a *son* to God.[2]

In order to attain this state we need to establish perfect control[3] of our mind and our desires. Not only must they be controlled, they must be made to dwindle to nothing. We also need perfect control of our physical visions and perceptions. We need perfect control of the five elements, the sexual energies and sexual fluids, and of the world within. All these various aspects have to shrink to nothing. One in whom all these are reduced to nothing is a *shaikh*. He is a Sufi *shaikh*, one who can guide the way and show the path. Such is the state of Sufism, the state of '*Sūfi-son*'. But if these things have not been brought under control and reduced, then he is only in the state of *sūpi*,[4] not Sufi.

Just as everything born in the world must die, just as everything that appeared must disappear—if one is truly in prayer, everything that has manifested within him must die in that prayer. That is true prayer. When he prays to God, when he worships God, everything that appeared within him must die.

However, if one holds onto his faith in those things and evokes them, placing them in front of him and worshiping them, that is not prayer. If one makes a form of the monkey that is within the mind and worships it, that is not prayer. If the elephant that is the arrogance within the mind is manifested outwardly and worshiped, that is not prayer. It is only an inner animal that is manifested and prayed to outside—an inner elephant, or dog, or snake, or monkey. This is not prayer. Only when all these things have died can you call it prayer. Only when the world as we perceive it and all the animals within us have been made to die is it true prayer. The prayers prayed in this state are called Sufi prayers, and this state is known as Sufism.

This, my brother, is what we are trying to learn here. It is this that my

---

2. *Sūfi-sun:* Bawa Muhaiyaddeen is punning on the word Sufism and the two English words, sun and son.

3. The word translated from Tamil as 'control' is *odukkam* which can also mean shrinkage, contracting, or being brought into a state of abeyance.

4. *sūpi:* This is a pun on the word Sufi. *Sūpi* is a Tamil word meaning a baby's pacifier, which provides temporary comfort but not any nourishment.

children and I are trying to practice. This is why we wake them up at such an early hour.

My brother, when fields and crops need to be irrigated, it is the overseer's duty to open the gates that will release water from the storage tank. But each farmer is responsible for channeling the water to his own field. He must do that for himself. The one who opens the main sluice will not divert the water to the individual fields. The same holds true in Sufism. It is my duty to open the gates and allow the water to flow out, a little at a time. But it is each person's responsibility to direct that water to his own field and cultivate it. That is not my responsibility.

At this time, at four a.m., the mind is dull and in a state of torpor, a feeling similar to the torpor experienced right after a meal. We feel tired and want to sleep. Again at about eleven a.m. or noon, we tend to feel tired and are unable to think clearly. This feeling comes in cycles, just as hunger does.

In the early morning, around three a.m., satan, the world, and the elements press down upon us and try to keep us drowsy. At such times we have to shake ourselves free and wake up. That is our duty. This is why prayers have been instituted at these early hours.

Man cannot truly pray until the mind has been controlled and subjugated. Before he can pray, the mind must die, and the world within him must die. Only if all that he holds within him dies can he maintain this other state. All the burdens he has loaded onto himself must be unloaded before he can take on something new. As long as he holds onto what he is carrying, there will be no room to take on something of greater benefit. If he can unload the kingdom of hell, if he can make it die and leave him, then the kingdom of heaven can come into him. Only if the five elements are unloaded can God come into him. My brother, to accomplish this in our lives is Sufism.

The Sufi prayer is *lā ilāha, illallāhu:* Other than You there is nothing else, You are Allah. This is the true prayer. In this prayer, a sound (not heard outwardly) should form at the tip of the tongue without the tongue actually moving. It is similar to the playing of a flute. Further, the *lā ilāha* and *illallāh* should work like the heart, pumping and resting, closing and opening, contracting and relaxing. The opening of the heart is *lā ilāha,* and the closing is *illallāh.* As the breath goes in and out, it follows the rhythm of the opening and closing of the heart. As the heart opens, we breathe out, and as it contracts, we breathe in. As it opens, the prayer is *lā ilāha:* Except for You there is nothing. You alone exist. This is the point. All other things are subject to disappearance. They are born and they perish, but You are Allah. *Lā ilāha:* I am not. All these things around me are not real. There is nothing other than You. As the heart contracts, the prayer *illallāh* must go in. *Illallāh:* You are Allah.

You must establish that power in the heart. Just as those in Islam face toward the west, you must point your wisdom and faith toward the power that is God. Then, joining with it, you must draw it along on the incoming breath to the accompaniment of *illallāh* and establish it in the right side of the heart. So, *lā ilāha* rides up on the breath that is exhaled through the left nostril, while *illallāh* rides in on the breath that enters through the right nostril. These are the words of the Sufi, "I am not. Only You are. Other than You there is nothing. You alone are God." This affirmation is prayer. The proof of this state comes when the 'I' is not, when the 'I' dies, when the world does not exist, when nothing exists except God. That is prayer. In this prayer, we prostrate to Allah 43,242 times each day, with each breath we take, at every moment, while we walk or sit, whether we are happy or sad, asleep or awake, reading or speaking.

In what way should this occur? Just as a man's heart goes on pumping as he goes about all his activities, so this breath of prayer should be constantly moving through his body. This is the prayer pump. His faith is the magnet of remembrance, pointing toward that power. That remembrance must keep on pumping within him, no matter what he is doing. The work we do in the world is a function of the mind, while our prayer is our faith and certitude in truth. Working toward the truth is the work of the right hand, while working in the world is the work of the left hand. Although these are separate functions, it is possible for both to be operating simultaneously. Just as the heart goes on pumping automatically, prayer must also go on at all times. Thus both kinds of work, the work in the world and God's work, must go on at all times, in conjunction with the flow of the breath. Understanding this and abiding by it is Sufism.

Unless one becomes a *Sūfi-sun* and gives light to the world, his prayer will not be true prayer. In the world, as the seasons change, only the sun, by the light it sheds, will know what is occurring in different places. Similarly, only if one has become a sun, only if one's wisdom, truth, and prayer have attained that state, can he understand what God and prayer really are. Until then he cannot understand. This is what is meant when people speak of Sufism. Therefore, my brother, it would be good if these children could learn this kind of prayer.

Now, say a person is learning to drive. Once he learns to steer the car, then with practice he may be able to drive. But it is not enough just to be able to drive the car; he must be able to read the map, know the route he has to take, and also know the mechanism of the car. If he is not familiar with the parts and how they work, he will not know what to do if the car stalls. The cause may be a blocked pipe or a loose nut. Only if he has the know-how will he be able to detect the problem, fix it, and be on his way. Otherwise, he will be stranded.

Similarly, in Sufism, teaching you just to drive is not sufficient. You must also know the inner workings and the route you need to take. It is for this reason, my brother, that my children and I are practicing this form of prayer. We are all learning. We say, *"Lā ilāha,"* and *"illallāh. Lā ilāha, illallāh."* This sound must come from within the movement of the breath. It is like a song played by a flute; the music comes from the instrument, not from the flutist's voice. Or for example, a guitar-player has a certain song in mind, and it comes out through the guitar as he plucks the strings. The music comes from the guitar, not from the guitarist. The nerves and blood vessels in your body are like the guitar strings. When they are strummed with *īmān* [faith, certitude, and determination], they must vibrate with the melody *lā ilāha, illallāh*. This sound must come forth from every one of the 4,448 blood vessels in the body, from the 248 bones, from the ligaments, the nerves, the muscles, and even from the blood. It must emanate from the 105 million hair follicles and pores of the skin. The sound of *lā ilāha, illallāh* must come forth from every single part of the body. It must come forth without your actually making a sound. This should go on continually, just as the heart does.

Because every minute part of the body vibrates with that sound, eight hundred million sounds of prayer resonate from your body with every breath. You are saying just this one word, but it is resonated by 800 million parts of the body. It is as though 800 million mouths are saying that word. The breath that went out is just one, but inside you, all the nerves, the blood vessels, the skin, the bones, the tissues—every one of the 800 million parts within you resonate to that sound. Only when that word is said with this kind of power can it be called Sufism.

You must draw each breath in that state. It is not just saying words with the mouth. Now say it with me: *"Lā ilāha, illallāh."* Faith must move with the breath, dive into God, and draw that power in through the right nostril. *Lā ilāha, illallāh. Lā ilāha, illallāh.* Then drop the sound and continue with only the movement. Keep on breathing in this way.

Bawa Muhaiyaddeen demonstrates. A short silent dhikr follows. Dawn breaks and the birds are chirping. Bawa Muhaiyaddeen continues:

Now the day is dawning. As the sun rises over the ocean from below the horizon, it looks red, like blood or fire. This is a time of turmoil. There is a magnetic force within the earth that has a connection within man. As the sun rises, the red fire mingles with the blood, and man's mind goes up and down, drawn and pulled by this magnetic force. This force pulls on his blood ties and attachments.

Within man there is a world, and there is also the world on the outside. Within man there is an ocean of illusion [*māyā*], and outside there are oceans formed of water. Within him there is a sun and a moon, and there is also a sun and moon on the outside. As the sun rises, its energy [*shakti*] pulls on him. And just as the sun possesses a blood-red color when it rises and sets, so man holds on to numerous blood ties and attachments, both when he is being born and when he is dying. This is the significance of the red color.

Sufis are not affected by these inner attachments. For a Sufi, all these have died. He has made them die. There will be no pull on him, because no such connection exists in him. Just as a magnet cannot exert a pull if there is no iron, a Sufi cannot be dragged by the world if he has no world within him. But as long as the world continues to exist within a man, it will have that magnetic pull. Therefore, it is not good to pray when that pull is active, because during this time, he is prone to turmoil. If the world is still within him that pull will occur, and he should not continue his prayer. He is like iron being pulled by a magnetic current. If, however, he becomes like a log of dead wood, the current cannot pull on him or draw him toward it. Such a one can pray at any time. For him all twenty-four hours are a time of prayer, and so this restriction does not apply. But for those who still retain any iron that can be dragged by the magnetic current—their prayers must be at the prescribed times. Only Sufis can continue beyond this time. For all others, prayer just after sunrise can result in chaos. They will not find peace at that time.

If we want to understand what prayer really is, we must first understand how to pray, how to conduct ourselves, how to say the prayers, and how to bring them within.

For instance, in the mosque, the call to prayer is given in a loud voice. *Allāhu akbar:* God is great! People respond to the call and go to the mosque for prayer. When the prayer begins, again *Allāhu akbar* is said, but this time the sound is not as loud. When the congregation bows in *rukū‘* the sound becomes even less, and when they prostrate themselves the sound is still quieter.

Much like that, the sound in the *sharī‘at* form of prayer is loud, but as you progress, gradually the sounds grow quieter and quieter. Similarly, while doing the *dhikr,* when you say, "*Lā ilāha,*" the sound can be heard. When you say, "*Illallāh,*" the sound becomes less, until finally there is no sound. Although you may be aware of the motor of the *dhikr* running, you will not be aware of the current as it passes through.

Now, electricity exists within the five elements (earth, fire, water, air, and ether). As long as it is intimately mingled with them, we can safely touch the earth or the water. However, once the electric current is extracted it becomes dangerous, and if the elements in our body touch it, it can shock us and fling us away, or even kill us. In this state, electricity and the elements are no longer the friends they once were.

The *dhikr* works in a similar way. In the body, this prayer-current is intimately mingled with the five elements. If we succeed in completely extracting the prayer-current from the elements, this body will be transformed into pure current, into light. It will become a 'current-city.'[5] If any element makes contact with it at this point, the current will shock us and fling us far away.

We need to extract the prayer-current. But we must not touch it as long as we have any connection to our body of the five elements, or it will shock us and fling us down. That current moves within our body without our being aware of it, just as electricity flows invisibly through copper wires. We can see the insulated wires, but we cannot see the current that passes through them, so there is no way of knowing whether it is flowing, unless we use a voltage tester. Even then, we will not actually feel the electricity, we will only see a glowing light on the instrument.

---

5. 'current-city': Bawa Muhaiyaddeen is punning on the word electri-city.

Prayer is like that. The current may be flowing, but to prove it is there we need to affix the correct bulb and switch it on. The switch (faith in God) makes a connection to the bulb (which stands for God) via this prayer that flows along the nerves and blood vessels. The prayer will be flowing, but no one else will be aware of it. It is not something one can perceive through touch or sight. One who tries in this way will not find it.

So, do it like this. First say, *"Lā ilāha,"* audibly, and then *"illallāh"* with a softer sound. As you go on practicing it, the sound will grow softer and softer. Later, when it begins to run automatically with the breath, your prayer will be so imperceptible that no one will be aware of it except God, the wire, and the current that flows through the wire. No one else will know.

This is true prayer. As you go on doing the *dhikr,* the prayer will continue to flow along automatically, unseen, like the electric current in a wire. It cannot be shown to others. But if someone who holds on to the elements within him tries to touch it, he will know, for it will hurl him away.

My children, this is what the prayer of a Sufi is like. Once it has been extracted, it will flow along easily. The light will be imperceptible to others, but it will be seen by God. A true *kāmil shaikh* will also be able to verify whether the prayer is flowing or not.

Our prayer must attain this state. All twenty-four hours this Sufi prayer must go on without ceasing. Both negative and positive currents can be functioning simultaneously throughout the day. The negative is our duty to the world. The positive is prayer, our duty to God. Both are necessary. Both have to keep working. One current should work in one direction, the other in a different direction. Do not try to run them together or let them contact each other. If you do, it will start a fire. Each must go its own way. Then there will be only light. This is true prayer. This is the prayer we must practice, the prayer of Sufis. Every child must perform this prayer in the proper way.

It was necessary for me to speak at length today about prayer, even though it may have interrupted the meditation that some of my children wanted to do. I could speak even longer, but my brother has work to do, so we should not detain him too long. I had to speak because I saw a thought in my brother, "What is this thing called prayer? What does prayer really mean? How should it be done?" Because I saw these questions within him, I had to give this long explanation.

What is prayer? To whom does one pray? True prayer occurs only when God prays to God. That is real prayer. *Lā ilāha:* Nothing else but You. *Illallāh:* You are God. In that state you become God and pray to God. That is the word.

Once something has been recorded on tape, it is not necessary for a person to be there to speak. The tape itself will emit the sound of his voice. In the same way, if one has surrendered to God, if he has recorded himself onto God, then God Himself will play back that sound.

February 1, 1978

CHAPTER FIVE

The Power of the Dhikr

While doing the dhikr, *Bawa Muhaiyaddeen explains what is happening at each step.*

Whthen you are learning to practice the *dhikr* initially, you will say it audibly, in a speaking voice, as I am doing now. *Lā ilāha, illallāh; lā ilāha, illallāh.* This remembrance must rise up on the breath, just as the air comes forth from the lungs. First you say *lā ilāha:* Nothing other than You. Next, when you say, "*Illallāh:* You are Allah," the sound is softer. With practice, it becomes progressively softer until it comes to settle on the tip of the tongue. At that point, when you say, "*Lā ilāha,*" there is no sound, only a fine movement of the tip of the tongue.

When you are drawing the breath in, a slight trembling of the right eyelid occurs. A gentle inward drawing of the right eye is also felt as it pulls the *dhikr* in. This is how it must be done.

Bawa Muhaiyaddeen demonstrates.

The tip of the tongue experiences a fine movement up and down. The skin pores, the hair follicles, and the nerves should be aware of the movement and sound of the *dhikr.* It must seep into every minute particle of the body. Awareness must be following its movement and also be conscious of the skin pores opening their mouths as they proclaim the *dhikr.*

Try to draw in the breath in this way. See if you are aware of the movement of the *dhikr.* The hair follicles on the scalp and all over the body must open their mouths and recite, "*Illallāh,*" and this should be known to awareness. Their sound should be heard by the ears and heard within. It should sound like a hum.

By now the breath has become gentler, finer. Its movement has become less, slower. At this point wisdom has merged with the remembrance of the word, while the *dhikr* has merged with the breath. The breath is becoming connected with the life, the soul [*rūh*]. Now only the meaning, the mystery, and the soul are functioning. There are no longer any sounds.

Only the soul is working. The *dhikr* is flowing along with the soul. What-ever one may be doing, that *dhikr* remains connected to the soul, to life. And, since life pervades every part of the body, making every part of the body function, the *dhikr* also pervades the whole body—the hands, legs, fingers, toes, and nails. Now you can feel the beat of the pulse through-out the body.

At this stage you have eyes in front of you, behind you, to the right, and to the left. You can see on all sides. There will be light everywhere. Normally the eyes see only in front, but now they can see behind, to the left, and to the right. Even if you close your eyes, that wisdom will allow you to see in all directions.

You will be able to see the nerves, the bones, and every part of your body. You will see what they look like and what they are doing. All of these can be seen as though your body were made of glass. It is the eye of wisdom that can see this. You can observe the air shifting around in the body; you can see how the breath moves and how the blood flows. Wis-dom is able to see how every part of the body functions. When you look at the upper part of the body, you will see inside your head and view the workings of the brain. And if you look with wisdom you will be able to see the *'arsh, kursī, qalam,*[1] heaven, and earth. Wherever wisdom directs its attention, each thing will be seen immediately. Wisdom, or conscious-ness, is the 'seeing eye'. Wherever you take this eye of consciousness, it will explain with discernment all that you see. As you ask within, "What is this? What is the point to learn from this?" it will give all the mean-ings: "This is this, this is that," and so on.

If you say you want to see America, it will be seen, no matter where you may be. If you want to see the house of one of these children, as soon as the thought arises, that house will be shown, as well as the various rooms in it and how many people are there. The explanation will be received by the inner heart [*qalb*], and wisdom will see. Everything you might want to know about the sky, the earth, and the netherworld—all will be shown.

If you want to know something about a person, everything will be seen as if through a transparency. As soon as a thought arises, wisdom will point out to you what you want to see. Everything can be seen in this

---

1. *'arsh:* The throne of God, on the crown of the head.
   kursi: The gnostic eye, at the center of the forehead; the *qutbiyyat* eye.
   qalam: The divine pen; the pen with which Allah has prerecorded the actions of human beings.

way. Allah and the *Rasūl* ﷺ can be seen, but not as a form. Allah will be seen as a power and the *Rasūl* ﷺ as a resplendence. If you want to bring something to life—be it earth, sky, or even a corpse—whatever you intend, it will stand before you. As soon as you have that thought, and say, "Rise!" it will rise. And, having given life to it, you can talk with it. You can ask it whatever you want, and the answers will be received in the innermost heart [*qalb*]. You will see the form, you will see the mouth moving, and the reply will be received in that inner heart.

Such is the power of this *dhikr*. The greatness of it is beyond description. You must develop it until you reach this state and obtain its benefits. Every one of the 43,242 breaths per day must do this *dhikr*. If each one of you will do this, then whatever it is you are seeking will be yours. But as long as you do not attain this state in your *dhikr*, if determination and tenderness and this state are not present, it will not be this kind of *dhikr*.

In this state, there is no need to bow down in prostration. Even when you are seated—if you form the intention, the soul will do whatever prostration has to be done. You will not have to actually place your forehead on the earth, for the forehead will be resting on Allah. The prostration must be done to Allah Himself. As soon as the intention arises in you, the *dhikr*—that inner form—must go and make contact with Him.

This is the *dhikr* of *Lā ilāha*: There is nothing other than You. *Illallāh*: You alone are Allah. It is a prayer in which the 'I' does not exist, and God prays to God. This is the true state of the *dhikr*. There can be no substitute for this.

February 3, 1978

CHAPTER SIX

Become One with God

My loving children, you need to reflect on each explanation of the *dhikr* and the ways of worship [*'ibādat*] and prayer. There are millions of ways to worship God. But God is One. He is a treasure which cannot be seen by mind and desire. He has no form that can be perceived by His creations. He has no beginning or end. He is the perfection, the omnipresent treasure which is the eternal soul, a treasure without beginning or end.

Whatever worships God must also be formless and without beginning or end. Thus God can be seen and worshiped only by God's treasure. This treasure, which knows how God should be worshiped, is the wisdom of His essence [*dhāt*]. It has the capacity to discern and distinguish. It is the complete, all-pervading, resplendent wisdom known as divine luminous wisdom [*perr arivu*]. This resplendent wisdom is the *Nūr*. It is with this wisdom that one can know God and pray to Him.

Wisdom has no shadow.[1] The soul has no shadow. Everything else, all of God's creations have a beginning and an end. All things that have been born must come to an end. Anything that has appeared must disappear. All things created by man will also disappear. There is a time of destruction for all the gods and all the things created by man. Only God exists forever.

Therefore, it is not possible to worship God with this form which has been born and will end. Worship occurs only when the rays of the resplendent wisdom of grace that radiate from Him resplend as one with the soul and worship the One who is the resplendence within their resplendence. That is true worship, the worship that merges with Him.

We must search for, discover, learn about, and attain this resplendent wisdom from one who has it. Only the wisdom which can perceive God,

---

1. To cast a shadow, there must be a form. Wisdom and the soul have no form, hence no beginning or end. They are eternal. See also Glossary: *sadalam*.

the primal resplendence, can learn this wisdom. Whoever attains it will know this worship. It will not be found within any kind of divisiveness such as exists in races and religions and scriptures. Only perfect purity can see the perfect purity. To merge with one who has that purity is to become one with God and with the hearts of all lives. To worship in union with such a one is to see all lives as one. The prayer performed by the perfect wisdom of such a one is the perfection of divine knowledge [*gnānam*]. We must know that whatever worships God has to be God. Only that worship can understand and glorify God.

Any worship that is not done in this state will exhibit four hundred trillion, ten thousand differences and divisions. Such worship has been called by many names: prayer, *dhikr*, meditation, *mantras*, incantations, *pūjās*, occult feats, and magic tricks.

In these, millions of forms and shapes are created by mind and desire, given various names, and then prayed to with the recitation of *mantras* and incantations. The energies [*shaktis*] of earth, fire, air, water, and ether (the power of the mind) are thereby aroused by using the five letters, made to enter idols and statues, and then used to perform occult feats. But when these energies see the radiance of wisdom, which is the light of the soul, all the *mantras* and miracles become powerless, just as the glitters of the moon and stars are no longer visible when swallowed up by the brilliant light of the sun. We must understand this. God is the omnipresent completeness. No prison can enclose Him. He exists as wisdom within wisdom, in the form of love and grace. He is the original glory. The treasure that is seen within wisdom is God. We need to know this. He does not want or accept even an atom of the milk, fruits, coconuts, curd, rice, ghee, honey, sugar, or millions of other things we offer to Him in worship. He created us, and in His goodness, He gives food to us instead of accepting food from us. What will He accept from us? Truth, love, compassion, forbearance, tolerance, peacefulness, honesty, conscience, God's justice, the king's justice, man's justice, and the three thousand divine qualities—this is what He asks for, nothing else.

If, instead of these, we offer prayers, or *pūjās*, or ten million kinds of worship, even if we bore a hole in a rock and hide within it, Yaman, the Angel of Death, will still find us. Death will not spare us. Therefore, we must understand this and die before death. If we can make our mind and desire die, if we can end our connection to our blood ties, to creation, to earth, water, anger (which is fire), air, and ether (the thoughts of heaven and hell), then the world in us has died. When the world in us has died, there is no death for us. We have died before death. We have become that treasure which does not experience death, that treasure which is God. When the world is not, God is. If we have no attachments, we are God. If we have no connection to earth, to air, to our base desires, we are God. If we have no connection to water, to semen, we are God. If we have no connection to ether, to the energy of the monkey mind, we are God. If we have no connection to desire, we are God.

When all of these connections die, our state becomes omnipresent. Our life becomes all-pervasive. This is God's state, God's power. He has none of these connections, therefore He has no death. If we too can cut these connections, then there is no death for us. This state has to be understood.

This is what is known as dying before death. When one who has attained this state worships and prays to God, unites with God, and merges with God—that is the prayer of perfect purity.

In God's creation there are 105 million kinds of shadows of consciousness. Feeling, awareness, and intellect are in the form of that shadow. Millions of creations (worms, beetles, snakes, scorpions, etc.) function with just these three states of consciousness. They have feeling [*unarvu*] which causes them to wriggle when touched. They have an awareness [*unarchi*] of their surroundings and the intellect [*pudthi*] to escape. Their prayers function at the level of these three states of consciousness. What they do not have is the wisdom which analyzes with discernment.

Such creatures flock together in their own groups, guided by their intellect. The way these groups pray is limited by their level of consciousness, which goes only as high as intellect. Their mind and their learning function only up to that level. Their life of desires ends there also. Countless creations function like this, with only feeling, awareness, and intellect, and they worship with this kind of understanding. In this kind of worship one creation appears, then creates another and worships it. Thus one thing which will die worships another which is dying. If you have wisdom and examine this with discernment, you will come to know the treasure which never dies and was never created, which is without beginning or end, the all-pervasive Omnipresence beyond description, the One with the lone resonance of *illallāhu*, the unique One, the One who is alone.

If with wisdom you can realize this one treasure and worship it, this is the worship worth learning. You must acquire the wisdom necessary to learn this kind of worship.

Therefore, my children, take within your inner heart [*qalb*] the mirror of wisdom of the resplendence of grace. Within that mirror you will see the effulgence, and if you merge with that and become the effulgent light within that mirror, if you merge with the wisdom within wisdom, what you will see in that mirror will be God. He will be your form, and you will be His beauty. There will be no more world within you. Only He will be there. Not you, only He. Thus it is He who sees Himself, worships Himself, and merges with Himself. When the two are merged as one, and the one treasure sees the one Effulgence, when the one is merged with the One—that is true worship. Realize that you must make this worship your own. This is the resplendence, the highest point of the worship of God.

My children! You must understand this. You need wisdom. That treasure is the wisdom within wisdom. Therefore, learn wisdom. *Āmīn.*

May God protect and sustain us. With certitude and determination you must learn this wisdom and this worship, and you must adopt the prayer that merges with Him, the prayer in which He is within you and you are within Him. In this kind of worship the two are one. All other kinds of worship are for created things, which begin and end. When they end, the worship will end too. When the worshiped thing perishes, the worship perishes along with it.

We must understand this. *Āmīn.* May God, with His grace, grant us perfectly pure wisdom and this perfectly pure form of worship. May He protect and sustain us. May He make us merge as one with Him. Just as fire consumes water, may He consume us with His grace, and make us one with Him. *Āmīn. Āmīn. Al-hamdu lillāh!* All praise is due to Him. *Āmīn.*

June 15, 1974

Appendix 1

The Twenty-eight Letters within Man:
Explanation and Illustration

The following explanation and illustrations are excerpts from Guru Mani (Gems from the Guru) by M. R. Bawa Muhaiyaddeen, published in Tamil in 1961 and not yet available in English.

Allāhu taʿālā Nāyan created *Āthi Muhammad*. Within that He created the fourteen worlds. Within *Muhammad* He created the seven days, and within the seven days He created the seven *dēvas* [celestial beings], who are the seven planets. Then He made *Muhammad* into a peacock, and when He gazed at it with His look of grace, the body of the peacock began to melt. From the drops of sweat that fell from it, He brought forth the heavenly beings in the seven heavens. Then calling it, "O *Muhammad!*" Allah gazed intently at the peacock once again.

At this the peacock began trembling and screamed, "O my God! Because of Your gaze my whole body is falling apart piece by piece!"

Upon hearing this God said, "O My *Muhammad!* Using you I am going to create man. Now look at Me," and again He looked intently. Then the body of the peacock split into thirty-one pieces. God gazed at it once again with His eye of grace, and these pieces became thirty-one letters. He gazed at them intently, and of the thirty-one, three letters stood apart from the rest. Those three letters were *alif* (ا), *lām* (ل), and *mīm* (م). The remaining twenty-eight stood individually, separate from each other.

Then the peacock which is *Muhammad* asked, "O my God! What is the reason for three of the thirty-one letters, which are in my form, splitting off and standing separate?"

To this God replied, "O *Muhammad!* Of these three letters, I will be the eternally indestructible treasure which is *alif.* The letter *lām* will be *Āthi Muhammad*, the one who belongs rightfully to all of mankind. The letter *mīm*, O *Muhammad*, will be you. The two of you will shine as My two eyes, while I will shine as the eye in the middle of the forehead [the gnostic eye] for you. I will be luminous forever. I will always be the first crescent moon. No one's eyes will see Me, O *Muhammad!* You will shine as the second crescent moon. You will resplend from Me and reveal Me. A few will know you, but the majority will not. The third crescent, which is *Ādam (Sivan)* will be seen by all lives in the world. O *Muhammad!* We three will be letters forever indestructible. O *Muhammad!* The two of you will always exist along with Me.

"I am going to create mankind. I am going to use those twenty-eight letters that are standing apart from each other to create *Ādam*, or *Sivan*. I will place each letter in a particular place and form his body." So saying, Allah created *Ādam (Sivan)* using the twenty-eight letters.

Thereupon those letters screamed, "O our God! You have separated us and placed each of us by ourselves as stations within the human body! How can we be away from You?"

To this God replied, "Using you I have created *Ādam*, and I will dwell in his forehead. *Muhammad* will be on the bridge of his nose, and I will be *alif*, on his forehead. They will call Me 'Allah, God'. They will call the *lām* 'Āthi Muhammad'. *Ādam* will be the *rūh*, the soul, the father to all lives. From *Ādam*, I will create *Awwāl*, Eve or *Īswari* in order to propagate the world. Eve will be the eye, the letter *nūn* (ن). I will place the rest of you individually in twenty-five stations. I will make the twenty-seven of you shine on earth as twenty-seven stars. Of the twenty-eight letters, I will be on the forehead, *Āthi Muhammad* will be in the brain, *Muhammad* will be on the nose, *Ādam* will be the life [*rūh*], while the twenty-five of you will form the house in which We dwell." So said God.

Upon hearing this, the twenty-five letters asked, "O our God! Where will the three of You be, later?" God replied, "We will exist in both the worlds, here and there. Those who have the ability to see us will appear in the world very rarely. If they can see with clarity, they will see us both there and here. Once they see us, we will always remain with them, without ever leaving them. Apart from Me, the twenty-seven of you will radiate as twenty-seven stars. And the world will shower praise upon you."

Upon hearing this, the letters said, "O God! Even though we shine as stars, will man know that we are mingled within the human form?"

So that man may realize this, God created *Ādam*, impressed the pearl which is *Muhammad* on *Ādam's* forehead, and said, "By the light of that pearl they will see all things, and Me."

Within *Ādam* God created *Awwāl* (Eve), and from within *Awwāl* He created the prophets: Noah, Abraham, Ishmael, Moses, David, and Jesus (peace be upon them all). After these prophets had resplended as illumined beings, I brought forth *Muhammad*, sent down the 6,666 *āyāt* to him, gave him instruction, told him of your greatness, how you shone as stars in earlier times, how the twenty-eight letters formed the body of the children of *Ādam* and dwelt in the earth-world as stars. I explained all this to *Muhammad*, drew for him the human form using the twenty-eight letters, explained the greatness within you, your powers, the beauties of that form, and the greatness of man. When *Muhammad* emerges in a form, he will demonstrate your greatness and the beauty of the human form. I will be the great star, the resplendence which will never disappear, while you will shine as the lesser stars, which are the twenty-eight letters.

"Including Me, you are the twenty-eight letters within man's form. By yourself you are the twenty-seven stars. I have fashioned you into the twelve *rāsis* [zodiac signs], shining as the twelve *dēvas*, ruling the body as the twelve openings. Of these, nine openings are impure, while three have the purity to know Me. In order that human beings and other lives may know with clarity, We appear as follows: *Ādam* as the night of the new moon, *Muhammad* as the full moon, and I as the first crescent. The twenty-five of you dwell within Us. One who has seen Us will subdue and control you, while you will control one who has not seen Us. But I will explain Our secret, your secret, and the secret of creation to young *Muhammad*.

Muhammad appeared and disappeared many times and finally dawned in *Furqān*. Then the *Āthi* demonstrated with clarity to *Muhammad* what He had earlier discoursed to the stars and the *dēvas*, explained to him about the secrets of creation, showed him clearly the right ways to worship God, showed him the secrets of the four realms: earth, sky, this world, and the netherworld, and told *Muhammad*, "Tell of the wonder of My creation to every life and every thing I created, and make them aware of My glory."

The Locations of the Letters within the Body

Skull	*jīm*	ج
Brain	*mīm*	م
Forehead	*thā'*	ث
Right eyebrow	*tā'*	ت
Left eyebrow	*bā'*	ب
Eye	*nūn*	ن
Right ear	*ḍād*	ض
Left ear	*ṣād*	ص
Nose bridge	*alif*	ا
Throat	*lām*	ل
Right shoulder blade	*ḥā'*	ح
Left shoulder blade	*khā'*	خ
Two-way split in the throat	*yā'*	ي
Right foot	*ẓā'*	ظ
Left foot	*ṭā'*	ط
Spine	*kāf*	ك
Right rib cage	*rā'*	ر
Left rib cage	*zā'*	ز
Right breast	*shīn*	ش
Left breast	*sīn*	س
Right shoulder	*'ain*	ع
Left shoulder	*ghain*	غ
Right elbow	*fā'*	ف
Left elbow	*qāf*	ق
Navel	*wāw*	و
Seat (bottom)	*lām alif hamza*	لأ
Right kneecap	*dhāl*	ذ
Left kneecap	*dāl*	د

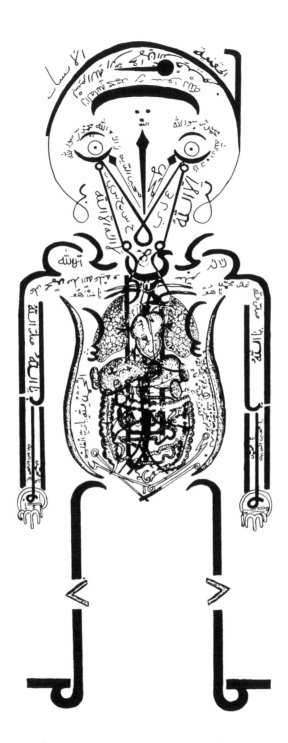

The human form made of the twenty-eight Arabic letters.

The Seven Realms within the Body

These seven powers [*shaktis*] climb up from the central portion of man's body, which is the chest, and exert their rule. If you want to learn of this, you must stay with a good *guru*, abide by his word, and do service to him. If you do, you will gain the ability to see these heavenly beings [*dēvas*]. You will also be able to commune with them. Listen, my son, while I tell you where these seven dwell.

> Jibrīl is in the liver.
>
> Mīkā'īl is in the spleen.
>
> Isrāfil is in the lungs.
>
> 'Izrā'īl is between the liver and the bile (gall bladder).
>
> Iblīs is in the bile (gall bladder).
>
> The Emperor Muhammad dwells in places beyond description.
>
> God (the King of kings) dwells between the nose and forehead.

These dwell as the seven sages [*rishis*]. Having established rulership in the seven realms above, they abide in the six-cornered house in the central realm which is the chest, or heart. They function as rulers for the seven realms above, for which the Emperor Muhammad functions as the minister and God as the overall Ruler, the King, while iblīs rules the seven realms below which are hell.

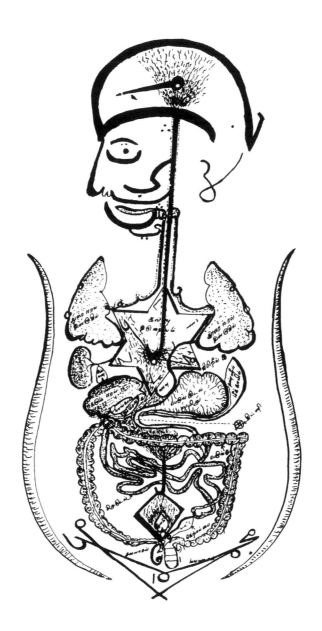

The inner instruments for the emergence of *gnānam*
(divine wisdom). The light that is formed by the raising
and lowering of the *dhikr* is *gnānam*.

Appendix 2

The Nine Muhammads

Bawa Muhaiyaddeen has related the hadīth *in which God said, "O Muhammad, without you I would not have created anything." Therefore, we must understand who we are. The heart [aham] is Allah's treasury. The face [muham] is Allah's beauty. The two merged as one is* Muhammad. *Without these two, Allah would not have made anything into form. He would not have created anything without His essence [dhāt], without His beauty, His light.*

In this hadīth, *God was speaking about that light of* Muhammad *which has existed as Islam [purity] since the beginning, in the world of the souls [arwāh], and which will exist forever. For both the beginning and the end, Islam came in the form of unity through the* Muhammad *of the nine meanings.*[1]

Bawa Muhaiyaddeen gave the following definitions for each of the Nine Muhammads.

1. *Anāthi Muhammad*: The Unmanifested. The name Allah gives to the *Nūr*, God's resplendent light, in *anāthi*. *Anāthi* is the beginningless beginning, the time of profound silence, when nothing had been manifested and Allah existed as Himself, with the *Nūr*, as yet unmanifested, within Him.

2. *Āthi Muhammad:* The Manifested. *Āthi* is the primal beginning, when the essence [*dhāt*] of Allah emerged from Him. When His essence attained His beauty and came forth from Him, Allah saw it as light. The light He saw was His own face [*muham*], and He gave it the name *Muhammad*. This is *Āthi Muhammad.*

3. *Awwal Muhammad:* The Beginning. *Awwal* is the beginning, the emergence of creation. At this time Allah gave to the light of the *Nūr* the name *Awwal Muhammad.*

---

1. Bawa Muhaiyaddeen expounds upon this point in *Islam and World Peace: Explanations of a Sufi,* pages 99-103.

4. *Hayāt Muhammad:* The Eternal. The *rūh* [soul, or life] which exists forever; the truth which never dies.

5. *Anna Muhammad:* The Nourishment. *Anna Muhammad* comes as food and nourishment to each life. *Anna Muhammad* is all the different kinds of nourishment required by each of the six types of lives. It is the beauty that is Allah's grace, the nourishment of His grace. For *hayāt*, or eternal life, *Anna Muhammad* comes to the heart and the face as the nourishment which is Allah's beauty. The sole nourishment for the soul of man, or *hayāt*, is the beauty of Allah, which comes from His light in the form of atoms of His grace. For the other five types of lives, *Anna Muhammad* comes as the nourishment related to earth, fire, water, air, and ether.

6. *Ahamad:* The Heart. The light of the beauty of Allah's essence [*dhāt*], which is the inner heart, called *aham*, or *qalb*.

7. *Muhammad:* The beauty of the light of Allah's essence, His heart, reflected in the face.

8. *Nūr Muhammad:* The Plenitude. The light which became complete within Allah and then emerged from within Him. The beauty and the light of Allah's three thousand gracious qualities; the light of His benevolent qualities of patience; the radiance of Allah's essence, or *dhāt*, which shines within the resplendence of His truth. It was the light of *Muhammad* called *Nūr Muhammad* that was impressed upon the forehead of Adam ☙. Of the nine aspects of *Muhammad*, *Nūr Muhammad* is the aspect of wisdom.

9. *Allāh Muhammad:* The light of Allah within *Muhammad* and the light of *Muhammad* within Allah. The name that Allah gives to *Muhammad* when the limitless resplendent *Nūr* once again sees the Perfection, Allah, from which it originally emerged. Having come forth from that Perfection, and manifested all of creation, that light once again lost itself in that original source. Thus the two became one, and Allah called this *Allāh Muhammad*. What is called *Muhammad* is a vessel within which Allah resides and from within which He speaks. Of the nine aspects of *Muhammad*, *Allāh Muhammad* is the highest; *Muhammad* is completely merged in Allah, existing only as a vehicle for the

manifestation of His essence and attributes. Only the pretext of Muhammad's ﷺ form is there; because Allah is formless, the form of Muhammad ﷺ appears to exist so that the perfect beauty and grace of the Invisible can be seen.

Appendix 3

The Inner Meaning of the Seven Diacritical Marks

The Arabic alphabet consists of twenty-eight letters, all of which are consonants. Several of the consonants look alike but are differentiated by one, two, or three dots, called a nuqat, *which appear above or below the letter. The vowels, of which there are seven, take the form of diacritical marks. The* fathah (´) *gives the sound 'aaa', the* maddah (˜) *lengthens the* fathah, *the* dhammah (ˀ) *gives the sound 'uuu', the* kasrah (ˍ) *gives the sound 'eee', the* sukūn (°) *indicates that no vowel is applied, the* shaddah (˜) *makes it a double consonant, and the* wasil (˞) *indicates that the* alif *is not pronounced.*

These notations are not necessary for people who speak Arabic fluently, and they are frequently omitted entirely. However, they are included in the Holy Qur'an in order to avoid any misinterpretations. In a mystical sense, the diacritical marks are said to give life to the letters which would otherwise be silent. Bawa Muhaiyaddeen expounded upon this mystical explanation in the following talk given expressly for this book.

In the *Qur'ān*, there are seven diacritical marks. These give rise to the various sounds such as 'aaa' from the *fathah* and 'uuu' from the *dhammah*. Allah formed these seven diacritical marks from the essences of the seven levels of wisdom. Through these seven sounds which are His essences, Allah gave life to the *Qur'ān* which is His grace. There is a very deep meaning connected to these marks.

Consider the *nuqat* and the *sukūn*. The *nuqat* represents Allah's intention. Allah, the One of limitless grace and incomparable love, extracts just one dot from that grace and love. When Allah places that dot, that *nuqat*, that intention, and with His pen which is the *alif*, the dot becomes a small circle which is the *sukūn*. That *sukūn* contains all of everything in the entire creation. Allah says, "*Kun!* Be!" and awakens all of everything in the eighteen thousand universes and the fifteen realms. That is the *sukūn*. Allah is the *alif*, the pen; the *nuqat* is His intention; and the *sukūn* is the three worlds: *awwal, dunyā,* and *ākhirah* [the world of the souls, this world, and the hereafter]. With the word *"Kun!"* Allah gives them life and causes them to arise. This is also how man is awakened.

Allah's intention is just one dot of His essence. Everything that is created originates from this *nuqat,* and the meaning contained within it is now called the *Qur'ān.* The rest of His limitless grace and incomparable love remains within Him. He extracted only one dot from all that, gave it life, and through it revealed all of everything.

Allah gave the explanation contained within this *nuqat* to the 124,000 prophets. In the *Qur'ān,* Allah speaks of twenty-five prophets as the most eminent; of these, eight became His representatives; and of them, Muhammad ﷺ was made the Messenger and given the title of *rahmatul-'ālamīn,* the mercy for all the universes. Allah said, "You are the emperor to My *rahmat."* The 6,666 verses of the Holy Qur'an and the traditions [*ahādīth*] which were within the *nuqat* were all revealed and explained to *Muhammadur-Rasūl* ﷺ.

The twenty-eight letters were also contained within the *nuqat.* Together these letters formed the *Qur'ān,* and they also constitute the form of man, the *sūratul-insān.* Thus, the form of man is the *Qur'ān.* But these letters were silent, and it was through the seven basic principles that this form of man, this *Qur'ān,* was given life. Through these seven, the 6,666 verses were given sound, sent down as His commandments, and explained to the prophets.

Allah's kingdom, Allah's house, Allah's *Qur'ān* was placed within the heart of Muhammad ﷺ. It was to this heart, to this *Qur'ān,* that Allah's commandments were sent. But without these seven essences, no sound can come forth from the *Qur'ān* of Allah's grace. It is silent. Through these seven essences, Allah reveals Himself.

In the same way, the form of man, the *sūratul-insān,* was given seven sounds: feeling, awareness, intellect, assessment, subtle wisdom, divine analytic wisdom, and divine luminous wisdom. Just as the seven basic principles gave sound to the *Qur'ān,* these seven can awaken that sound within the *sūratul-insān.* They can make the twenty-eight letters resonate within the form of man and reveal Allah to him. They help him understand good and evil [*khair* and *sharr*], the essence and the creation [*dhāt* and *sifāt*], night and day, and life and death. All such things are explained through the seven basic principles.

The *Qur'ān* has to be brought to life through these seven in order for man to understand the mystery of his innermost heart, his *qalb*. The heart of man is the *Qur'ān*; it is the *Sūratul-Fātihah* and the *Sūratul-Ikhlās*.

> *Qul hūwallāhu ahad*—to all of everything, Allah is
>   the *ahad*, the One, the Absolute.
> *Allāhu samad*—the One who belongs equally to all
>   creations.
> *Lam yalid*—He is the One responsible for the pro-
>   tection of the right and the left. He is the
>   great One to a great one and a devotee to a
>   devotee.
> *Wa lam yūlad*—the One who exists always in truth.
> *Wa lam yakul-lahu*—the One who is in all of everything
>   as the omnipresent plenitude.
> *Kufuwan ahad*—He is the *ahad*, the mystery, to all of everything.

These seven sounds must be awakened within man in order that he may understand the *Sūratul-Qur'ān* which is the *sūratul-insān*, the *qalb*.

Without these seven principles there would be no sound, the *Qur'ān* would not be understood, and there would only be darkness, the darkness that existed in *anāthi* [the time before creation when Allah was alone]. Only when these seven are aroused is man truly brought to life. Only then will he be known as *Nūr Muhammad*, *Ahamad*, *Anna Muhammad*, and *Hayāt Muhammad*. It is through these seven principles that these states can be known.

The *Qur'ān* and the *ahādīth* are within man. If these seven are not awakened, the letters within the body of man will not have life and his *Qur'ān* will be closed. Without sound, without life, without goodness, man will be like a corpse.

These seven principles are for the *Qur'ān* and for the form of man. In order for each letter to be brought to life, we have to know which principle or diacritical mark needs to be placed where. The *nuqat*, *fathah*, *dhammah*, *kasrah*, etc. need to be placed accurately for the letters to awaken. Only then will the sounds come alive and that grace be known. Only then will the light dawn and the plenitude prevail. Only in that state of pleni-tude can man, as Allah, converse with Allah and be given a place in His kingdom.

In the *Qur'ān*, Allah has revealed these seven principles as the diacritical marks, and in the form of man He has revealed them as the seven levels of wisdom. With His pen, the *alif*, Allah placed His intention within only one dot of His limitless grace. With the *sukūn* and with the word *"Kun!"* He caused all of everything to awaken. We should understand this meaning. This is only a brief explanation.

September 11, 1975

Appendix 4

*Sūratul-Fātihah and Sūratul-Ikhlās
with Commentary from the Yusuf Ali
Translation of the Holy Qur'an*

Sūratul-Fātihah, or the Opening Chapter:[18]

1. *Bismillāhir-Rahmānir-Rahīm.*
   In the name of God, Most Gracious, Most Merciful.[19]
2. *Al-hamdu lillāhi Rabbil-'ālamīn;*
   Praise be to God,
   The Cherisher and Sustainer[20] of the Worlds;
3. *Ar-Rahmānir-Rahīm;*
   Most Gracious, Most Merciful;
4. *Māliki yaumid-dīn.*
   Master of the Day of Judgment.
5. *Iyyāka na'budu wa iyyāka nasta'īn.*
   Thee do we worship,[21]
   And Thine aid we seek.
6. *Ihdinas-sirātal-mustaqīm,*
   Show[22] us the straight way,
7. *Sirāt al-ladhīna an'amta 'alaihim,*
   Ghairil-maghdūbi 'alaihim wa lad-dāllīn.
   The way of those on whom
   Thou hast bestowed Thy Grace,
   Those whose (portion)
   Is not wrath,[23]
   And who go not astray.[24]

---

18. By universal consent it is rightly placed at the beginning of the *Qur-ān,* as
summing up, in marvelously terse and comprehensive words, man's relation to

God in contemplation and prayer. In our spiritual contemplation the first words should be those of praise. If the praise is from our inmost being, it brings us into union with God's will. Then our eyes see all good, peace, and harmony. Evil, rebellion, and conflict are purged out. They do not exist for us, for our eyes are lifted up above them in praise. Then we see God's attributes better (verses 2-4). This leads us to the attitude of worship and acknowledgment (verse 5). And finally comes prayer for guidance, and a contemplation of what guidance means (verses 6-7).

God needs no praise, for He is above all praise; He needs no petition, for He knows our needs better than we do ourselves; and His bounties are open without asking, to the righteous and the sinner alike. The prayer is for our own spiritual education, consolation, and confirmation.

That is why the words in this *Sūra* are given to us in the form in which we should utter them. When we reach enlightenment, they flow spontaneously from us.

19. The Arabic words *"Rahmān"* and *"Rahīm,"* translated "Most Gracious" and "Most Merciful" are both intensive forms referring to different aspects of God's attribute of Mercy. The Arabic intensive is more suited to express God's attributes than the superlative degree in English. The latter implies a comparison with other beings, or with other times or places, while there is no being like unto God, and He is independent of Time and Place. Mercy may imply pity, long-suffering, patience and forgiveness, all of which the sinner needs and God Most Merciful bestows in abundant measure. But there is a Mercy that goes before even the need arises, the Grace which is ever watchful, and flows from God Most Gracious to all His creatures, protecting them, preserving them, guiding them, and leading them to clearer light and higher life. For this reason the attribute *Rahmān* (Most Gracious) is not applied to any but God, but the attribute *Rahīm* (Merciful), is a general term, and may also be applied to Men. To make us contemplate these boundless gifts of God, the formula: "In the name of God Most Gracious, Most Merciful": is placed before every *Sūrat* of the *Qur-ān* (except the ninth), and repeated at the beginning of every act by the Muslim who dedicates his life to God, and whose hope is in His Mercy.

Opinion is divided whether the *Bismillāh* should be numbered as a separate verse or not. It is unanimously agreed that it is part of the *Qur-ān*. Therefore it is better to give it an independent number in the first *Sūra*. For subsequent *Sūras* it is treated as an introduction or head-line, and therefore not numbered.

20. The Arabic word *Rabb*, usually translated Lord, has also the meaning of cherishing, sustaining, bringing to maturity. God cares for all the worlds He has created.

There are many worlds,—astronomical and physical worlds, worlds of thought, spiritual worlds, and so on. In every one of them, God is all in all. We express only one aspect of it when we say: "In Him we live, and move, and have our being." The mystical division between (1) *Nāsūt*, the human world knowable by the senses, (2) *Malakūt*, the invisible world of angels, and (3) *Lāhūt*, the divine world of Reality, requires a whole volume to explain it.

21. On realizing in our souls God's love and care, His grace and mercy, and His power and justice (as Ruler of the Day of Judgment), the immediate result is that we bend in the act of worship, and see both our shortcomings and His all-sufficient power. The emphatic form means that not only do we reach the position of worshipping God and asking for His help, but we worship Him alone and ask for His aid only. For there is none other than He worthy of our devotion and able to help us. The plural 'we' indicates that we associate ourselves with all who seek God, thus strengthening ourselves and strengthening them in fellowship of faith.

22. If we translate by the English word "guide," we shall have to say: Guide us to and in the straight Way." For we may be wandering aimlessly, and the first step is to find the Way; and the second need is to keep in the Way: our own wisdom may fail in either case. The straight Way is often the narrow Way, or the steep Way, which many people shun (xc.11). By the world's perversity the straight Way is sometimes stigmatized and the crooked Way praised. How are we to judge? We must ask for God's guidance. With a little spiritual insight we shall see which are the people who walk in the light of God's grace, and which are those that walk in the darkness of Wrath. This also would help our judgment.

23. Note that the words relating to Grace are connected actively with God; those relating to Wrath are impersonal. In the one case God's Mercy encompasses us beyond our deserts. In the other case our own actions are responsible for the Wrath, the negative of Grace, Peace, or Harmony.

24. Are there two categories?—those who are in the darkness of Wrath and those who stray? The first are those who deliberately break God's law; the second those who stray out of carelessness or negligence. Both are responsible for their own acts or omissions. In opposition to both are the people who are in the light of God's Grace: for His Grace not only protects them from active wrong (if they will only submit their will to Him) but also from straying into paths of temptation or carelessness. The negative *ghair* should be construed as applying not to the way, but as describing men protected from two dangers by God's Grace.

Sūratul-Ikhlās, or Purity (of Faith):

1. *Qul: Huwallāhu ahad;*[6296]
   Say: He is God,
   The One and Only;[6297]
2. *Allāhus-samad;*
   God, the Eternal, Absolute;[6298]
3. *Lam yalid, wa lam yūlad;*
   He begetteth not,
   Nor is He begotten;[6299]
4. *Wa lam yakul-lahu kufuwan ahad.*
   And there is none
   Like unto Him.[6300]

6296. The nature of God is here indicated to us in a few words, such as we can understand. The qualities of God are described in numerous places elsewhere, *e.g.*; in lix. 22-24, lxii. 1, and ii. 255. Here we are especially taught to avoid the pitfalls into which men and nations have fallen at various times in trying to understand God. The first thing we have to note is that His nature is so sublime, so far beyond our limited conceptions, that the best way in which we can realize Him is to feel that He is a Personality, "He", and not a mere abstract conception of philosophy. He is near us; He cares for us; we owe our existence to Him. Secondly, He is the One and Only God, the Only One to Whom worship is due; all other things or beings that we can think of are His creatures and in no way comparable to Him. Thirdly, He is Eternal, without beginning or end, Absolute, not limited by time or place or circumstance, the Reality before which all other things or places are mere shadows or reflections. Fourthly, we must not think of Him as having a son or a father, for that would be to import animal qualities into our conception of Him. Fifthly, He is not like any other person or thing that we know or can imagine: His qualities and nature are unique.

6297. This is to negative the idea of Polytheism, a system in which people believe in gods many and lords many. Such a system is opposed to our truest and profoundest conceptions of life. For Unity in Design, Unity in the fundamental facts of existence, proclaim the Unity of the Maker.

6298. *Samad* is difficult to translate by one word. I have used two, "Eternal" and "Absolute." The latter implies: (1) that absolute existence can only be predicated of Him; all other existence is temporal or conditional; (2) that He is dependent on no person or things, but all persons or things are dependent on Him, thus negativing the idea of gods and goddesses who ate and drank, wrangled and plotted, depended on the gifts of worshippers, etc.

6299. This is to negative the Christian idea of the godhead, "the Father", "the only-begotten Son" etc.

6300. This sums up the whole argument and warns us specially against Anthropomorphism, the tendency to conceive of God after our own pattern, an insidious tendency that creeps in at all times and among all peoples.

Appendix 5

The Seven Levels of Consciousness

In the book Questions of Life—Answers of Wisdom, *Bawa Muhaiyaddeen has explained that what is called wisdom is not a simple thing. There are seven levels of wisdom, or states of consciousness: feeling, awareness, intellect, assessment, or judgment, subtle wisdom, divine analytic or discerning wisdom, and divine luminous wisdom.*

All lives have the first three levels: feeling, awareness, and intellect. Using these three, when they are pricked they feel it and wriggle, and when something bites, they are aware of its location and know to brush it away. These three levels are present in animals, in snakes, in grass and weeds, and even in insects.

Man possesses these three levels of consciousness, but he also possesses four levels above and beyond these: assessment, subtle wisdom, divine analytic wisdom, and divine luminous wisdom. With these God has given the human being a connection to Him. He has placed His kingdom within the human being and the human being within His kingdom through these seven levels. How is it revealed?

The words of the prophets first come to feeling, then feeling explains it to awareness, and awareness conveys each message to the intellect. We receive them with our intellect and then follow them. Beyond that is judgment or assessment which we use to evaluate our life. The Qutb functions as the higher levels of wisdom, going beyond intellect to deeper and deeper levels, and as we grow in wisdom, it shows us the meaning at each step, point by point. First as subtle wisdom, it helps us to see and understand the subtlety within each different point. Then, as divine analytic wisdom, the Qutb explains what this is and what that is and then analyzes the difference between them. Finally it becomes divine luminous wisdom, the Nūr. That is the completeness which says, "This is His power."

For this book, Bawa Muhaiyaddeen gave the following definitions of these seven states of consciousness:

1. *Unarvu:* Feeling, or perception. With perception, man inquires into his actions and the meaning of his life. In addition, by placing his feeling within the feelings of other lives, he will understand the state God has given to that life. On the physical level, *unarvu* is sensory perception,

which informs a person, for example, that something is crawling on his foot.

2. *Unarchi:* Awareness. With awareness, man locates and pinpoints his feelings and perception and inquires into himself. Also, by sending his awareness to mingle with the awareness of the countless creations, he can understand their consciousness and know what they are aware of. On the physical level, *unarchi* informs us of the location of the sensations felt by *unarvu.*

3. *Pudthi:* Intellect. Intellect is the cognitive ability of the five elements. It is the essence of the understanding gained through feeling and awareness. It emerges from them and has control over them.

4. *Mathi:* Assessment, or judgment. At this level, man estimates the realm that his soul emerged from [*awwal*], the realm of this world [*dunyā*], and the realm of the hereafter [*ākhirah*]. It assesses his life, his body, and his wisdom.

5. *Arivu:* Subtle wisdom. The five elements of earth, fire, water, air, and ether can function only up to the third level, which is intellect. Only man possesses the fourth level, assessment. *Arivu* is the subtle wisdom that arises from the essence of his assessment, his ability to assess things.

6. *Pahuth arivu:* Divine analytic wisdom. This wisdom emerges from the essence of subtle wisdom, or *arivu.* It is the wisdom which distinguishes between right and wrong and takes only what is right. It cuts away the illusions of the elements and explains the truth of God. It exists as atom within atom in man and opens up and analyzes everything—what a man sees, hears, smells, tastes, and feels; what he intends, dreams, and realizes; heaven and hell; the plenitude of God. This sixth level of wisdom is known as *Muhaiyaddeen* and *Qutbiyyat.*

7. *Perr arivu:* Divine luminous wisdom. This wisdom emerges from the *Qutbiyyat.* It is God's greatest gift to man, the divine luminous wisdom that allows him to realize that he exists within God, and God exists within him. At this seventh level, man totally surrenders to God *tawakkul-'alallāh.* This is the wisdom of the *Nūr.* The light that resplends from it is Allah.

Glossary

The following traditional supplications in Arabic calligraphy are used throughout the text:

ﷺ following the Prophet Muhammad or *Rasūlullāh* stands for *sallallāhu 'alaihi wa sallam*, may the blessings and peace of Allah be upon him.

؏ following the name of a prophet or an angel stands for *'alaihis-salām*, peace be upon him.

؉ following the name of a companion of the Prophet Muhammad, a saint, or *khalīfah* stands for *radiyallāhu 'anhu* or *'anhā*, may Allah be pleased with him or her.

(A) Indicates an Arabic word

(T) Indicates a Tamil word

(U) Indicates an Urdu word

(P) Indicates a Persian word

'abd (A) Slave; a slave of God; one who is completely surrendered to the service of God.

Ādam-zāth (A & U) Those who have the form of Adam ؏; mankind; human beings; children of Adam ؏.

ahad (A) The only One; referring to God in His absoluteness.

ahādīth (A) (sing. *hadīth*) In Islam, authenticated accounts relating the deeds and utterances of the Prophet Muhammad ﷺ. Words of wisdom; discourse of wisdom. *See also Hadīth qudsī.*

aham (T) The inner heart, or *qalb*.

Ahamad (A & T) *Ahmad* (A) The sixth of the nine *Muhammads;* the light of the beauty of Allah's essence [*dhāt*], which is the inner heart, called the *aham*, or *qalb*.

ākhirah (A) The hereafter; the next world; the kingdom of God. The returning to and disappearance of each thing in the place it originally came from is *ākhirah*. *Ākhirah* is one of the three worlds—*awwal* [the beginning of creation], *dunyā* [this world], *ākhirah* [the hereafter]. When the *rūh* disappears into the world of souls, that is *awwal*. And when it disappears into the world [*dunyā*] and into satan, that is hell. But when the *rūh* [soul], the treasure that came from Allah, disappears into that with which it should merge, into Allah, then that is *ākhirah*, the hereafter.

ālam (A) (pl. *ālamīn*) A world; cosmos; universe. There are eighteen thousand universes within the *qalb* [innermost heart]. This world [*dunyā*] is a universe, an *ālam*. Heaven is one universe, hell is another. There are also the universe of the soul, the universe of angels, the universe of jinns, of fire, of earth, of water, of air, of fairies, of satan, of the prophets, of the saints, of the *qutbs*, of wisdom, of the *Nūr*, and of Allah. There are even the universes [*ālamīn*] of birds, worms, reptiles, and snakes. There are also *al-ʿālamul-arwāh* and *al-ʿālamul-ajsām*. *ʿĀlam* is that which is revealed; *ajsām* is the unrevealed. Everything beyond these is *arwāh*.

ʿālamul-arwāh (A) The world of pure souls where all souls are performing *tasbīh*, or prayers of glorification to God.

al-hamdu lillāh (A) All praise belongs to God. All praise for everything that has appeared and everything that comes to an end is due to God alone. When you say, "*Al-hamdu lillāh*," you praise Him saying, "Everything is Yours."

Al-hamdu Sūrat (A) The Chapter of Praise. Another name for *Sūratul-Fātihah*, the opening chapter of the Holy Qur'an.

alif (A) The first letter of the Arabic alphabet [ﺍ]. To the transformed man of wisdom it represents God, Allah. There is a beginning and an end, but Allah alone is eternal, existing forever naturally as the natural reality. For Him there is no beginning, end, or destruction. He alone is Allah, *alif*. Then and now He alone exists.

Allah, *Allāhu* (A) God; the One and Only. The words Allah and *Allāhu* are very similar except that Allah simply refers to Him, whereas *Allāhu* calls to Him with a great depth of feeling. "You, O Allah, are the explanation and the resonance. Everything emerges from You. Both the explanation and the resonance come from You. The sound of "*hū*" exists in You." That is *Allāhu*.

Allāh Muhammad (A) The ninth of the nine *Muhammads*; the light of Allah within *Muhammad* and the light of *Muhammad* within Allah. *See also* Appendix: The Nine *Muhammads*.

Allāhu akbar! (A) God is great!

Allāhu ta'ālā (A) God is the Lord above all. *Allāhu:* Almighty God. *Ta'ālā:* the One who exists in all lives in a state of humility and exaltedness.

Āmīn (A) Amen; so be it; may He make this complete; may it be so. All praise belongs to Allah alone. There is no praise other than the praise of God. The praise of a worthy heart can be only for Him.

ān (T) Male. Allah alone is male. Everything that was created is female. Those who praise Him, find joy in Him, and ask Him for favors are female. Only Allah, His grace, and His light are male [*ān*].

anāthi (T) The period without limit, before the beginning. In *anāthi* everything was there, but there was no sound, no manifest indication that anything existed. Thus *anāthi* is the stillness of silence, *mounam*. *Āthi* is the time in which God's power is revealed. It is the beginning of sound, revealing that something is there. God's resplendent light, the *Nūr*, emerges, and the darkness is dispelled. *Awwal* is the time when all creations are brought forth through the power revealed from God, the time when things are manifested and seen. Thus, in *anāthi*, God is alone, meditating on Himself. In *āthi*, His light, the *Nūr*, emerges from His heart. The *Nūr* and *Qutbiyyat* rub against each other and bring forth the souls. *Āthi* is the time of the emergence and scattering of the souls. *Awwal* is the time when those souls glorify Allah and take form. Allah first created the forms and then placed the souls within them.

Anāthi Muhammad (T & A) The Unmanifested; the first of the nine *Muhammads*; the name given to the *Nūr*, God's resplendent light, in *anāthi*, the beginningless beginning. *See also* Appendix: The Nine *Muhammads*.

Āndavan (T) God.

Anna Muhammad (T & A) The Nourishment; the fifth of the nine *Muhammads*. *Anna Muhammad* is the one who comes as food and nourishment to each life. *See also rizq* and Appendix: The Nine *Muhammads*.

arivu (T) Subtle wisdom; the fifth level of wisdom or consciousness. *See also* Appendix: The Seven Levels of Consciousness.

'arsh (A) The throne of God; the plenitude from which God rules; the station located on the crown of the head which is the throne that can bear the weight of Allah. Allah is so heavy that we cannot carry the load with our hands or legs. The *'arsh* is the only part of man that can support Allah. Allah is the all-pervasive omnipresent effulgence of wisdom within wisdom. The light called

Nūr is the plenitude of wisdom, and that is the throne on which the power which is Allah sits.

'arshul-mu'min (A) The throne of the true believer [*mu'min*]. There are two thrones for Allah within man. One is his innermost heart, the seat of his perfectly pure certitude of faith [*īmān*], the throne called *Īmān-Islām*. The other is the plenitude of wisdom, which is the light of the *Nūr*. Allah resides in the light of this plenitude and rules from there.

arwāh (A) (sing. *rūh*) The invisible divine realm; the station where Allah resides. Lit. souls; light rays of God.

asmā'ul-husnā (A) The ninety-nine beautiful names of Allah. These ninety-nine are the names of His qualities [*ismus-sifāt*], while the one hundredth name, Allah, is the name of His essence [*ismudh-dhāt*]. Of His three thousand divine attributes, these one hundred were given in their completeness to man.

The *asmā'ul-husnā* is the form [*sūrat*] for Allah's divine names which are His plenitude. This is the true form of man [*sūratul-insān*] the one in which the 6,666 *āyāt* are placed. Ninety-nine of these divine names are within man, and they are also within Allah, for they are contained within the one-hundredth name.

'asr (A) The afternoon prayer; the third *waqt* of the five times prayer of Islam. This also represents the period when one should understand an important aspect of wisdom—the secret that exists between *dunyā* [this world] and *ākhirah* [the hereafter]. One should understand this between the ages of thirty and forty. This is the third *waqt* of his life. The first period is the time of his birth, the second is his time of growth, and the third is the time of his maturity. During this period of life, one must understand the significance of choosing to become one with Allah or of becoming one with the world. This is *'asr*.

as-salāmu 'alaikum, wa 'alaikumus-salām (A) The greeting, "May the peace of God be upon you," and the reply, "God's peace be with you too." Usually, these words are spoken casually, but when the *Nūr* emerged from Allah in *āthi* [the primal beginning], the *Nūr* paid obeisance and greeted Allah saying, "*Yā Allāh*, You are the only One who is perfect purity, Islam. The truth that is in You is Islam. *As-salāmu 'alaikum.* Whatever You created in *awwal* is the perfect purity of Islam. I too am Islam. The *īmān* [faith, certitude, and determination] that created beings have in You is also Islam. That which separated from You and will return to You is *Īmān-Islām. As-salāmu 'alaikum.* When what separated from You returns to You and purity joins with purity, it is Islam. When the treasure that separated from You reaches You, accepts You, and merges with You eternally, then it is Islam."

āthi (T) The primal beginning; the time when God becomes aware that there is something within Him; the time when the *Nūr* [the plenitude of the light of Allah] and the *Qutb* [the wisdom which explains the truth of God] manifest within Allah; the time of the dawning of the light; the world of grace where the unmanifested begins to manifest in the form of resonance. *Āthi* is the time when the first sound or vibration emerges, and the souls are formed. *Awwal* follows this and is the time when the creations become manifest in form. *See also anāthi*, which is the unlimited period before the beginning of the primal creation.

Āthi Muhammad (T & A) The Manifested; the second of the nine *Muhammads*. *Āthi* is the primal beginning, when the essence [*dhāt*] of Allah emerges from Him. *See also* Appendix: The Nine *Muhammads*.

āthi param jōthi (T) The effulgent Soul, that which is outspread in perfect completeness everywhere, existing within all lives in the form of light. That is Allah.

awwal (A) The time of the creation of forms; the stage at which the soul becomes surrounded by form and each creation takes shape; the stage at which the souls of the six kinds of lives (earth-life, fire-life, water-life, air-life, ether-life, and light-life) are placed in their respective forms. Allah created these forms and then placed that entrusted treasure which is the soul within those forms. *See also anāthi.*

Awwāl (T) Eve ⌣. *See also Pārvathi.*

awwal fajr (A) The *fajr* or *subh* prayer is the early morning prayer prayed just before sunrise. The *awwal fajr* prayer, also called *tahajjud*, comes before this prayer. An important part of this prayer is the supplication [*du'ā'*] called *qunūt*, recited just before the *sujūd* in the final *rak'at*. Reciting the *qunūt* is a duty for everyone. This *du'ā* prevents Dajjāl [the Antichrist] from escaping from the mountain within which he is buried. Dajjāl's hands and feet are bound in chains. During the night, he tries to lick his way out of the mountain and by four a.m. he has almost reached the surface. The *qunūt* prayer causes the mountain to grow around him, thus burying him deep inside once again.

Awwal Muhammad (A) The third of the nine *Muhammads*; the Beginning; the emergence of creation. *See also* Appendix: The Nine *Muhammads*.

āyat (A) *(pl. āyāt)* A verse in the Holy Qur'an; the words of Allah.

Badushāh (U) A king. The title of *Badushāh* is also used for Allah, the King of kings, the Lord of all kingdoms; the One who protects and nourishes.

bahrul-'ilm (A) The ocean of divine knowledge.

Bismillāhir-Rahmānir-Rahīm (A) In the name of God, Most Merciful, Most Compassionate. Allah is the *Rahmān* [Merciful One] and the *Rahīm* [Compassionate One] who creates, protects, and sustains all three worlds. This is Allah's duty. He alone can do this. *Allāhu ta'ālā Nāyan* has no beginning or end. The *bismin* resonated within Him and came from Him. Allah is One of limitless grace and incomparable love. Anyone who recites His *bismin*, this *kalimah*, with firm certitude and faith will receive the treasures of all three worlds [*awwal*, *dunyā*, and *ākhirah*], the treasure of *gnānam*, the treasure of grace, and the treasure of wisdom and divine knowledge [*'ilm*]. To those who intend Him, Allah gives what they intend. This word was written on the tablet in the world of the souls [*arwāh*].

Bismillāhi—In the name of Allah; the cause for all things which have a beginning and things which do not have a beginning.

ar-Rahmān: He is the King, the One who gives food, the Nourisher, the One who showers compassion on all creations equally; the One who protects all creations; the beneficent One.

ar-Rahīm: He sustains all creations. On the day of inquiry and the Day of Judgment the final redemption is in Him. He gives judgment to each creation according to what they have done.

chakkaravarthi (T) A great king; an emperor. Allah is the King of kings, the King of all the eighteen thousand universes.

chandira kalai (T) The art of controlling the breath. *Sūriya kalai* [the sun breath inhaled on the right side] is the breath of divine analytic wisdom. It is the breath of the *qutbiyyat*, or light, the breath of divine wisdom. *Chandira kalai* [the moon breath exhaled on the left side] is the breath of the world. It belongs to the world and is the breath of the seven colors: earth, fire, water, air, ether, mind, and desire. *See also kalai gnānam.*

daulat (A) God's imperishable wealth; the true wealth that exists forever.

dēvas (T) Celestial beings.

dhāhuth (P) The throne of Allah; the *'arsh;* the kingdom of heaven from which Allah gives judgment. The station from which Allah cautions each of us through revelations and subtle warnings, "What you did was wrong. Go and ask for forgiveness."

dhāt (A) Allah's essence; His treasury of grace.

dhikr (A) The remembrance of God; to melt like wax in the light and power of God; devotion to God and remembrance of God in relation to each one of His ninety-nine gracious attributes.

With various intentions, the *dhikr* can be recited thirty-three times, one hundred times, five hundred times, one thousand times, ten thousand times, or one hundred thousand times, requesting and appealing to God through any one of the ninety-nine qualities, and the result will be in proportion to the intention. But of the many *dhikrs*, the most exalted *dhikr* of all is to say, "*Lā ilāha, illallāhu*—there is no god other than You. Only You are Allah." All the others relate to His *wilāyāt*, or His actions, but this *dhikr* points to Him and to Him alone. It is the communication with God, which runs as speech within speech, as breath within breath, and as soul within soul. If, through the wisdom of the *qutbiyyat*, one can bring this *dhikr* into the soul, causing it to travel along with the breath, then the *dhikr*, the wisdom, and the soul would ascend and descend in union, as one, 43,242 times a day.

If the soul runs like this, as *lā ilāha, illallāhu*, rising and lowering in this manner, then that is true prayer. Then, having transcended the 'I', all desires having died, needing nothing, and having the *īmān* of absolute certitude that only Allah exists—in that state one will be able to realize God. Of all the *dhikrs*, this is the *dhikr* of Allah's *'arsh* [the throne].

adh-dhikrul-jālī (A) The remembrance of God recited audibly. Reciting like the birds is known as *adh-dhikrul-jālī*.

adh-dhikrul-qalbī (A) The remembrance of God in the heart.

adh-dhikrur-rūhī (A) The remembrance of God by the life, or soul.

dīn (A) The pure light. *Dīnul-Islām* is the beauty of the pure light. Perfect purity, its light, and its truth are known as *dīn* and *dīnul-Islām*. This is the truth, the beauty and light of the truth, and the light of the truth for *dunyā* and *ākhirah*. Lit. religion; faith; path.

dīnul-Islām (A) *See dīn.*

dunyā (A) The alluring earth-world in which we live; the world of physical existence; the world of the five elements that exists both within and outside the body; the shadow-form of the five elements that exists within the body; the darkness which separated from *Nūr Muhammad* at the time when that light of *Nūr Muhammad* emerged from within Allah.

ejamān (T) Master. The *ejamān* of the soul or truth is Allah; the *ejamān* of bad qualities is satan, the master of hell.

Faqīr Muhaiyaddeen Mujāhidatullāh ☺ (A) The *Qutb* for this age. *Faqīr*—a poor man. In Sufism, a title for one who has reached the end of the spiritual path. *Muhaiyaddeen*—the giver of life [*hayy*] to pure faith [*dīn*]. *Mujāhidatullāh*—one who has steadfast determination on the path to Allah.

fard (A) (pl. *furūd*) Obligatory duty; to understand the rules and commandments of Allah, accept them, and act accordingly. In Islam there are five obligatory duties [*furūd*] known as the five pillars: 1. *ash-shahādah* [witnessing that there is no god but God, and Muhammad is the Messenger of God], 2. prayer, 3. charity, 4. fasting, and 5. holy pilgrimage [*hajj*].

Furqān (A) The scripture corresponding to the religions of Islam and Judaism. Lit. the criterion which distinguishes between good and evil, permissible and prohibited, truth and illusion. *See also Zabūr.*

ghee (T) Clarified butter usually made by melting butter, cooling it, and then extracting the more liquid portion.

gnānam (T) The wisdom of perfectly pure light; divine luminous wisdom.

guru (T) A spiritual teacher or guide; a *shaikh.* Bawa Muhaiyaddeen uses the word in the highest, purest sense, not to be confused with the many so-called teachers who descended upon the United States in the sixties.

Hadīth qudsī (A) Words of communion between Allah and Muhammad ﷺ, without the intermediary of the Angel Gabriel ﷺ. Allah's commandments and their meanings that every heart [*qalb*] knew in the beginning and understood, according to the capacity of its level of wisdom. *Hadīth:* Lit. traditions and sayings of the Prophet Muhammad ﷺ.

hajj (A) Holy pilgrimage to Mecca; the fifth of the five obligatory duties in Islam. All who are able to do so, financially and physically, should perform this pilgrimage at least once in their lifetime. Before they leave, they must give away their wealth and surrender all inner desires and ambitions. They must die to the world and meet God.

halāl (A) Those things that are permissible or lawful according to the commands of God and which conform to the word of God.

haqīqat (A) The third step of spiritual ascendance, signifying becoming close to Allah and the realization of divinity and the beginning of communion with God.

harām (A) That which is forbidden by truth, by justice, and by the warnings or commands of God. For those who are on the straight path, *harām* means all the evil things, the actions, the foods, and the dangers that can obstruct that path.

hayāt (A) In common usage *hayāt* means life, as when someone says, "May you have a long life." But *hayāt* really means eternal life. The soul [*rūh*] has *hayāt* [eternal life]. It never dies. It is imperishable. *Hayāt* can also be used to mean that one's *īmān* [absolute faith in Allah] has attained eternal life. When *īmān* becomes pure and eternal, it is *Īmān-Islām*. When someone says, "May you always be *hayāt*," he means, "May the purity which is *Īmān-Islām* remain alive in you without ever dying."

Hayāt Muhammad (A) The soul which exists forever; the fourth of the nine *Muhammads*; the truth which never dies. *See also* Appendix: The Nine *Muhammads*.

Hayāt Nabī (A) The Eternal Prophet; the Prophet of life, existing eternally as wisdom; the sixth level of consciousness within man.

hayawān (A) Animal; beast. The state of a human being in which his animal-like qualities dominate him.

hikmat (A) Divine wisdom. Lit. wisdom; judgment.

himmat (A) Perseverance; resolve; the faith and certitude to seek and meet with God. Those with *himmat* seek the path with faith and certitude. They focus on God with certitude and make the intention to undertake the journey despite all difficulties.

houris: This is an Anglicized word derived from the Arabic word *hūrīya* meaning celestial maidens. These are forms of grace which emerged from Allah's beautiful qualities; children whose qualities and beauty have acquired His grace. *Houris* have a very beautiful form and are always serving others. They are neither male nor female. They are the beneficent qualities of Allah, eternal, without birth or death.

hū (A) Within the heart, there is a sound which goes on resonating with the sound, "Hu, hu, hu, hu!" It is a resonance which never diminishes no matter how much we take from it. That resonance is *Allāhu. See also* Allah, *Allāhu*.

hubb (A) Love; to lose oneself in Allah. Desire shows duality, but to lose oneself and become one in the way that mercury is joined to the back of a mirror is a state of *hubb*.

'ibādat (A) Prayer, worship, meditation, and obedient service to the one God; to keep nothing other than Allah within the heart and to see only Him as God. There are many forms of worship. *Thiyānam* is to sit silently in meditation. *Thavam* denotes a deeper, more austere practice, such as praying and meditating without food or drink. *Dhikr* is the practice in which one raises and lowers the breath with the remembrance of God. *Fikr* is the concentration of one's thought and the intention for God along with the flow of breath. All these are methods of worship or prayer. Each word carries deep meanings. We have to

go deeper and deeper within the meaning of the word 'prayer'; our thoughts, our intentions, and our wisdom must go deeper and deeper. Our prayer is what we intend, what we understand and are able to see, and what is revealed in our heart.

Only the heart can pray with the knowledge of the connection between man and God. Only in the heart can the truth seek and find truth. That is true prayer, the intention and inner yearning for truth. That focus becomes associated with the breath; the breath connects with wisdom, wisdom joins with the light, and light merges with God. True prayer takes place only when one's yearning becomes so intently focused upon God that it does not forget God for even a second. The prayer connected to God in this fashion is the most exalted prayer.

Even if our breath is delayed, our yearning, our thought, and our intention must not be delayed. Before we begin to pray, our heart must have already begun to pray. Only when the heart is praying can we reach the state of seeking Him. We may go to a church, a mosque, or a temple, but first of all we must open our heart. Our intention and our *īmān* must worship Him.

If man achieves this state before he prays, then whatever prayer he performs becomes a most exalted prayer. But if man fails to clean the *musallā* [prayer mat] of his heart, then no matter where he goes to pray, it will not be true prayer. For, in that state, there are two. Only if he merges with God and prays as one will his prayer be true prayer. *See also dhikr.*

illallāh(u) (A) Nothing other than Allah. The second part of the *dhikr*, which accompanies the breath as it is drawn in through the right nostril and is finally deposited in the inner heart. *See also Lā ilāha, illallāhu.*

īmān (A) Absolute, complete, and unshakable faith, certitude, and determination that God alone exists; the complete acceptance by the heart that God is One.

Īmān-Islām (A) The state of the spotlessly pure heart which contains Allah's Holy Qur'an, His divine radiance, His divine wisdom, His truth, His prophets, His angels, and His laws. The pure heart which, having cut away all evil, takes on the power of that courageous determination called faith and stands shining in the resplendence of Allah. When the resplendence of Allah is seen as the completeness within the heart of man, that is *Īmān-Islām*. When the complete unshakable faith of the heart is directed toward the One who is completeness; when that completeness is made to merge within the One who is completeness; when that heart communes with that One, trusts only in Him, and worships only Him, accepting only Him and nothing else as the only perfection and the only One worthy of worship—that is *Īmān-Islām*.

īmān-kalimah (A) The affirmation of absolute faith in the one God: *Lā ilāha illallāh,*

Muhammadur-Rasūlullāh. None is worthy of worship other than Allah, and Muhammad ﷺ is the Messenger of Allah. Of the twenty-eight letters of the Arabic alphabet, which constitute the subtle body of man, twenty-seven comprise the form [*sūrat*] of the *īmān-kalimah.*

Injīl (A) Christianity. *See also Zabūr.*

insān (A) Man; a human being. The true form of man is the form of Allah's qualities, actions, conduct, behavior, and virtues. The one who has realized the completeness of this form, having filled himself with these qualities, is a true *insān.*

insān kāmil (A) A perfected, God-realized being; one who has realized Allah as his only wealth, cutting away all the wealth of the world and the wealth sought by the mind; one who has acquired God's qualities, performs his own actions accordingly, and immerses himself within those qualities.

'ishā' (A) The late night prayer; the fifth of the five times prayer of Islam. In one's life, *'ishā'* comes after one achieves a state like death, and the world within one's heart dies.

'ishq (A) Love; divine love; may also denote desire, depending on the context. There are two types of *'ishq.* There is physical desire which is known as *'ishq,* and then there is *hubb-'ishq* the love for and surrender to Allah. It is the surrender to the *lām,* or light. When it is the opposite of light, it is desire, but when it is the *hubb-'ishq* of light, it is the *'ishq* that has surrendered and disappeared in God. The *Rasūl* ﷺ was merged with Allah, and that is why they say the *Rasūl* ﷺ had *'ishq* for Allah. Love for Allah alone is *hubb.* It is the love that merges in God. If desire enters, there is a duality, but if one is merged with God, then there is only one, like the mercury on a mirror. This is *hubb. Hubb* means merging with God. However, because *'ishq* can be defined in several ways, it has to be defined according to the context.

Īswari (T) Adam ﷺ.

'Izrā'īl ﷺ (A) The Angel of Death; the angel of fire.

Jabrāt (A) The scripture corresponding to the religion of fire worship [Zoroastrianism]. *See also Zabūr.*

janāzah (A) Funeral prayers.

japa (T) Repetitive recitation of a prayer or *mantra,* usually done with beads.

Jibrīl or Gabriel ﷺ: The heavenly messenger who transmits divine wisdom; the archangel who brings the revelations of Allah. It is through Jibrīl ﷺ that Allah conveyed the *Qur'ān* to Prophet Muhammad ﷺ.

jinn (A) Subtle beings created out of fire. There are two kinds of *jinns*. Those formed in bad qualities are called satan's *jinns*. They do not glorify Allah. They create evil qualities. Those formed within obedience to Allah are different. They are perfectly pure and glorify Allah.

jum'ah (A) In Islam, the Friday congregational prayers held at midday.

kafan (A) The shroud used to wrap a corpse. It is a white robe which stands for purity. It is the robe of *īmān*, worn when *īmān* dawns after the death of the *nafs* [base desires].

kāfir (A) One who conceals Allah's truth; one who fails to live according to Allah's qualities and virtues although being aware of what Allah has commanded and forbidden; one who is ungrateful or who rejects Allah after having awareness of the truth, one who worships things as equal to Allah, falling under the power of his base desires. Such a one hides the truth out of purely selfish motives, turning the *qalb* into the form of darkness, falling prey to the force of satan, and acquiring the qualities of satan.

kalai (T) *Kalais* are all the arts and sciences through which man creates forms. There are sixty-four *kalais* [arts]. These include making forms such as statues and idols; using science to make forms, such as engines, motors, motorcycles, planes; performing circus acts, dance, games, physical exercise, and yoga; scenes seen with the eyes and scenes seen with the mind; acting, drama, and theater. Whether the result is flying in the sky, or walking on water, or controlling the breath, these are all *kalais*. It is acting upon what you have seen and dramatizing what you have looked at and learned. The four hundred trillion, ten thousand kinds of *siddhis* [magic tricks] are all included under *kalai gnānam*. Praying to statues and idols, or to water and earth, or to anything that relates to form, can be considered wisdom of the *kalais*, or *kalai gnānam*. It is a section of *agnānam*, which is ignorance, knowledge of the world and the elements. *Meignānam*, on the other hand, is true wisdom, which relates to the station of Allah.

kalai gnānam (T) The poetry, songs, and music of the world. *See also kalai.*

kalām (A) Word; God's word; the mirror of the ocean of His *'ilm* of grace; God's words of grace that shine as the resplendence of the Holy Qur'an.

kalimah (A) The affirmation of faith—*Lā ilāha, illallāhu:* There is nothing other than You, O God. Only You are Allah. The *kalimah* is Allah's grace and His pure light of truth, with which we can wash our *qalb*, or inner heart. That is the *awwal kalimah. Awwal* is the time that life appeared. The *kalimah* washes away all the *karma* that started from the time when each being was created, when each ray appeared and touched the world, resulting in bad qualities or *karma*. The *kalimah* washes all this away with truth. That is the *awwal kalimah*. This is a small meaning of the *kalimah*. The *kalimah* washes away all the faults and dirt that have been acquired in *awwal*, in the beginning of life. *See also dhikr; lā ilāha, illallāhu.*

kāmil shaikh (A) Perfect spiritual guide; the true guru; the one who, knowing himself and God, guides others on the straight path to Allah; one who has developed the three thousand gracious qualities of Allah.Sitting on the throne of patience, with the quality of compassion, the *kāmil shaikh* comforts his children and dispels the karmic evils of this world. He teaches them subtle wisdom. He teaches them about the form and makes them realize the form within the form. This form, or *sūrat*, is the light of the *Nūr*. He also shows his children the form and the light of *īmān* and shows that Allah is the wealth that exists within *īmān*.

karma (T) The inherited qualities formed at the time of conception. After the rays that were in Allah emerged from Him, satan's qualities appeared—the qualities of *māyā*, the qualities of desire, the qualities that are the essence of the five elements, the qualities of the mind, and all the thoughts, looks, and actions that arise from the connection to earth, to hell, and to *māyā*. These qualities form *karma*. What eliminates these from the body is the perfectly pure qualities of *īmān*, Allah's qualities.

kasthūri (T) The fragrance of grace that emanates from Allah's gracious qualities, from His good thoughts, from His form of beauty, from His *qalb;* the fragrance of His resplendent qualities. He gave this fragrance to Muhammad ⏤, comparing it to the fragrance of musk.

kātham kasthūri (T) Fragrant musk. This is the fragrance associated with Prophet Muhammad ⏤.

kathir (T) The rays of the *Nūr*, the light rays of Allah's grace [*rahmat*], which are the resplendent souls.

khair (A) That which is right or good; that which is acceptable to wisdom and to Allah, as opposed to *sharr*, that which is evil or bad.

khutbah (A) The sermon, or exhortation, delivered during the Friday congregation prayer [*jum'ah*]. When the *qalb* [innermost heart] is surrendered to Allah, when it prostrates to Him and hands over everything to His responsibility, when *īmān* becomes the resplendent light for the *qalb*, that *qalb* becomes Allah's church, or mosque. In that mosque, with lowered head and bowed heart, one must listen with divine wisdom to the words of Allah's *Rasūl* ⏤ and prostrate to God. This is the true meaning of *khutbah*.

kullum yāvum (T) All of everything. It refers to all the eighteen universes and the fifteen worlds.

Kun (A) Be!

kursī (A) The eye of wisdom [*gnānam*] in the forehead, the eye that exists between the two physical eyes is the gnostic eye. Lit. the seat of Allah's resplendence.

kursī gnānam (A & T) *See kursī.*

Lā ilāha, illallāhu (A) There is nothing other than You, O God! Only You are Allah. To accept this with certitude, to strengthen one's *īmān* [absolute faith], and to affirm this *kalimah* is the state of Islam. This is His unique, most exalted word. There are two aspects. *Lā ilāha* is the manifestation of creation [*sifāt*]. *Illallāhu* is the essence [*dhāt*]. All that has appeared, all creation, belongs to *lā ilāha*. The name of the One who created all that is *illallāhu*. Lit. No god (is), except Allah. *See also kalimah; dhikr.*

Lā ilāha illallāhu wa innī 'Īsā Rūhullāh (A) There is nothing other than You, O God! Only You are Allah, and Jesus is the soul of Allah.

Lailatul-Qadr (A) The Night of Power; traditionally the twenty-seventh night of *Ramadān* [the month of fasting]. The night the *Qur'ān* was sent down to the Prophet ⌣; the night when Allah's light, His grace, which is the *Thiru Qur'ān*, descended to the perfectly pure *qalb* of absolute faith [*īmān*]. Every light [*hayāt*] of the *Thiru Qur'ān* was sent down on that night to the heart free of darkness, the *qalb* of the *Rasūl* ⌣. At this time, God's explanations, all the letters and verses of the *Thiru Marai*, were sent as His grace in the form of rays to the *qalb* of the *Rasūl* ⌣. The *Qur'ān* is the light ray sent to a *qalb* which had no darkness, no *karma*.

lām (A) The Arabic letter (ل) which corresponds to the English consonant 'L'. *Lām* is the *Nūr*, or the light of the plenitude. It is divine luminous wisdom—the perfectly pure, seventh level of wisdom or consciousness.

maghrib (A) The sunset prayer; the fourth of the five times prayer of Islam; in the span of human life, *maghrib* is the state of one's death, when one's time in this world has finished. This word has one meaning in *sharī'at* and another in *ma'rifat*. In *sharī'at*, *maghrib* is the time of the prayer of sunset. But wisdom understands it differently. In *ma'rifat*, *maghrib* is a time when the world dies within oneself. It is a time when the darkness of the world is dispelled from one by wisdom.

mahr (A) Dowry. The dowry that Adam ☺ was asked to give was not money. He was asked to prostrate to Allah and offer his heart [*qalb*] in the presence of *Muhammadur-Rasūl* ☺ and the angels and heavenly beings, the four archangels Jibrīl, Mīkā'īl, Isrāfīl, and 'Izrā'īl, may the peace of God be upon them all, and the two angels on each shoulder, Munkar and Nakīr ☺. Each of us must give the bridal dowry of the *qalb* to Allah, the One of beauty, the only male.

mālik (A) King, referring to Allah.

mantra (T) An incantation or formula; the recitation of a magic word or set of words; sounds imbued with force or energy through constant repetition, but limited to the energy of the five elements. The *kalimah* is not a *mantra*.

ma'rifat (A) Gnosis, the fourth step of spiritual ascendance. *Ma'rifat* is a state in which there is no day and night, only light. It is beyond the ten sins. It is unity with Allah, intermingling with light, and existing in light always.

mathi (T) Assessment; judgment; the fourth level of consciousness. *See also* Appendix: The Seven Levels of Consciousness.

māyā (T) Illusion; the unreality of the visible world; a hypnotic fascination that arises within the form of darkness; the glitters seen in the darkness of illusion; the one hundred and five million glitters seen in the darkness of the mind which result in one hundred and five million rebirths. *Māyā* is an energy, or *shakti*, which takes on various shapes, causes man to forfeit his wisdom, and confuses and hypnotizes him into a state of torpor. It can take many, many millions of hypnotic forms. If man tries to grasp one of these forms with his intellect, although he sees the form he will never catch it, for it will elude him by taking on yet another form.

mayyit (A) Death. One who is born as a human being must die before his death. That death has three phases. 1. When he makes the world within him die, he causes the death of the five elements within his body. 2. When he makes desire [*nafs*] die, he becomes a true human being [*insān*]. 3. When he makes mind as well as desire die, he becomes a realized human being [*insān kāmil*]. Thus all three must die, in order for one to become an *insān kāmil*, a messenger, or representative of God. Lit. dead or inanimate.

mi'rāj (A) The night journey of the Prophet Muhammad ☺ through the heavens. It is said to have taken place in the twelfth year of the Prophet's mission, on the twenty-seventh day of the month of *Rajab*. Mi'rāj is when perfectly pure faith [*īmān*], wisdom, the beauty of the face [*Muhammad*], and the beauty of the heart [*Ahamad*] meet Allah and commune with Him.

mubārakāt (A) The wealth of the three worlds: the beginningless beginning [*awwal*], this world [*dunyā*], and the hereafter [*ākhirah*]. Allah's wealth is the wealth of the soul, the wealth of wisdom, and the wealth of His grace, which is the resplendent wisdom of the *Nūr.* Those who have received these three have received the *mubārakāt.*

Muhaiyaddeen or *Muhyiddīn* (A) The pure resplendence called the *Qutb.* The one who manifests the wisdom which lies hidden and buried under illusion [*māyā*]; the one who gives life to that wisdom and shows it again as a resplendence; the one who revives the life of wisdom and gives it to someone else. *Muhaiyaddeen: Mu* is that which existed earlier; *hayy* is life; *yā* is a title of greatness, a title of praise, and *dīn* means the light which is perfectly pure. *Dīn* is what existed in the beginning, the 'ancient thing' which was with God originally and is always with Him. To that purity God gave the name *Muhaiyaddeen.* *Muhaiyaddeen* is that beauty which manifested from Allah and to which Allah gave His *wilāyāt* [powers].

 Muhaiyaddeen is the perfectly pure divine analytic wisdom [*pahuth arivu*] which understands right and wrong, good and evil, permissible and prohibited, essence and form. The wisdom that discerns, distinguishes, and understands all of these is the *qutbiyyat,* the wisdom of *Muhaiyaddeen.* It takes what is *halāl* [lawful or permissible], discards everything else, accepts only Allah, and shows Allah to you. That is what is known as *Muhaiyaddeen* and *Qutb.*

muham (T) Face. Ordinarily, *muham* means the face. But within *Muhammad,* it means the beauty of Allah seen in the face, the beauty of the countenance.

Muhammad (A) The seventh of the nine *Muhammads*; the beauty of the light of Allah's essence found in the heart and reflected in the face. *See also* Appendix: The Nine *Muhammads.*

Muhammadiyyah (A) The station of *Muhammad.*

mujāhidatullāh (A) One who has steadfast determination on the path of Allah.

murīd (A) Disciple; one who follows and learns wisdom from one who has accepted Allah with absolute certainty and sees no god other than Allah.

nabī (A) A prophet. One who has accepted Allah's commandments and has surrendered to Him alone is a *nabī.* One who accepts Allah's commandments and covenants and does service to Him is a *nabī.* One who does the kind of service which can be rewarded only by Allah is a *nabī.*

nafs or *nafs ammārah* (A) The self-nature, soul, spirit, or essence of a thing. In Sufism, different levels of the *nafs* are delineated, from the lowest to the highest states of realization. The *nafs ammārah* describes the *nafs* at the lowest level, the level at which a person is motivated by base desires and cravings that are always saying, "I want this, I want that." There are seven *nafs*, or cravings, for the world. They are the essences of the world, of the five elements, and of mind and desire.

nāttam (T) Intention. *Nāttam* is to place one's heart in Allah's hands and to search for Allah alone. But if one makes satan responsible for his heart and yearns for the world, he will receive the earnings of the base desires [*nafs*].

niyyat (A) or *niyyatthu* (T) A firm intention or yearning for something; a vow. The intention of a true man is for Allah alone. He beseeches Allah alone and must receive only from Allah. Any intention for anything else is an intention for hell. It will be the intentions and aspirations of the mind and desire for the earnings of the world.

    Niyyat is the intention for God, the focus on God in every duty one undertakes. This intention [*niyyat*] is different from faith, certitude and determination and is not related to them (all these three).

nuqat (A) (sing. *nuqtah*) Dots (often used in this text to mean a singular dot); diacritical mark placed over or under certain Arabic letters to differentiate one from the other.

Nūr (A) Light; the resplendence of Allah; the plenitude of the light of Allah which has the brilliance of a hundred million suns; the completeness of Allah's qualities. When the plenitude of all these become one and resplend as one, that is the *Nūr*—that is Allah's qualities and His beauty. It is the resplendent wisdom which is innate in man and can be awakened. It is complete light, the light of Allah's grace, the light of God's essence, His *dhāt*.

Nūr Muhammad (A) The eighth of the nine *Muhammads;* the plenitude; the light which became complete within Allah and then emerged *See also* Appendix: The Nine *Muhammads*.

Nūr Muhammadiyyah (A) The light of the station of *Muhammad*.

pahuth arivu (T) Divine analytic wisdom; the sixth of the seven levels of consciousness. *See also* Appendix: The Seven Levels of Consciousness.

Paramasivan (T) The Tamil name for Adam ☙, the one who is the controller over the process of creation. Adam is the material from which creation is made: earth, fire, water, air, and ether. All five elements are contained within Adam. Therefore, Eve, or *Hawwā'*, had to be brought forth from this 'Adam', from a rib on his left side. Eve is *shakti*, the energy of earth. There is a saying: Adam ☙

is the sentient soul, or life [*jīvan*], and *Hawwā'* ⌣ is the energy [*shakti*]. Because Eve ⌣ was brought forth out of earth, Eve is the energy of earth, with its attributes, properties, and functions. Many, many energies are contained within the *shakti* that is Eve. One who has battled with and conquered all of these energies, one who has overcome the many energies connected with birth, is an *insān kāmil* [a perfected human being]. One who has transcended the state of an *insān kāmil*, one who has overcome that form, is a resplendent sun. One must transcend even this and go beyond. Once one does that, he is *Muhammad*. And when he realizes *Muhammad* and goes beyond, he is *Nūr Muhammad*. And when he realizes even *Nūr Muhammad* and goes beyond that, he is *Allāh Muhammad*. That beauty is a pure light which emerged from Allah Himself. It is a light that shines all over *awwal*, *dunyā*, and *ākhirah*, a light that lights up all three worlds.

Pārvathi (T) Eve: the partner of Adam ⌣. *Pār* is earth, or Adam. *Pārvathi* is the essence of the earth. *Pārvathi*, in Arabic, is *Hawwā'*, or Eve ⌣. It is the qualities of the earth, the four hundred trillion, ten thousand glitters and qualities of the earth. This is *māyā*. In Tamil they have given this different names: *Parāsakti*, *Pārvathi*, or *Paramēswari*. They have been called *Awwāl Amma*, *Hawwā' Amma*, *Amīnah Amma*, and *Wawamma*. *Amma* (T) means mother.

perr arivu (T) Divine luminous wisdom; the seventh of the seven levels of wisdom. *See also* Appendix: The Seven Levels of Consciousness.

porumay (T) Patience; a persevering, steadfast point [*himmat*] within God's power. It is a treasury within God's qualities, a bank where all treasures can be stored.

pudthi (T) Intellect; the third of the seven levels of wisdom: *unarvu* [feeling], *unarchi* [awareness], and *pudthi* [intellect]. *See also* Appendix: The Seven Levels of Consciousness.

pūjā (T) A ritual offering. One meaning of *pūjā* is making sacrifices and praying to the thoughts and intentions that arise from mind and desire. It is the prayers of mind and desire. Another meaning of *pūjā* is the worship of gods that the mind portrays. Man creates forms of the elemental spirits and of the thoughts that arise from the mind and then prays to them. People worship in many ritualistic ways; they light lamps, light candles, offer animal and human sacrifices, and offer fruits and coconuts. All this is *pūjā*. It is the worship of forms and idols.

But the worship of the one God does not involve *pūjās*, or ritualistic offerings. When mind and desire are both discarded, absolute faith goes into the soul, the soul goes into the *kalimah*, the *kalimah* goes into wisdom, the wisdom goes into the *Nūr*, and the *Nūr* goes into God and surrenders to Him and intermingles with Him. This is worship of the One. There is no *pūjā* for this.

qalam (A) The divine pen; the pen with which God is said to have prerecorded the actions of human beings. In the *ahādīth* of the Prophet ⊕, it is said that the first thing which God created was the pen [*qalam*] and that it wrote down the destiny of every individual thing to be created, all that was and all that would be, to all eternity.

qalb (A) Heart; the heart within the heart of man; the inner heart. There are two stations to this word. One is the four chambers of earth, fire, water, and air, which correspond to the four scriptures: *Zabūr, Jabrāt, Injīl,* and *Furqān.* The other station is within these four chambers. It is the *qalb,* the flower which consists of the qualities of Allah, the flower of His grace. This is the real *qalb,* the innermost heart. This *qalb* is the 'light' station, where only His fragrance exists. But the four chambers are dark and belong to the 'night' station, the black dog, called *kaluballā,* which is the world formed of the thoughts that belong to the five elements of earth, fire, water, air, and ether. Only when the beauty of God and His truth bloom in the heart does it become the station of the true *qalb.* It becomes the kingdom of God, His church, His mosque.

Some worship in the darkness, while others worship in the light. Those who worship within the beauty of God, worship in light. That is true prayer. That is the *qalb,* the heart. That is light. But those who worship in the four chambers worship in darkness, in night. Both are commonly referred to as *qalb,* but one is a flower, while the other is a dog. Many meanings can be given. This is just a brief explanation.

qiblah (A) The direction one faces in prayer. For Jews the *qiblah* is Jerusalem; for Muslims it is Mecca. Internally, the *qiblah* is the throne of God within the heart.

qudrat (A) God's benevolent grace. It is the wealth of grace from His three thousand gracious qualities which is given to those who have love and wisdom.

Qul: Huwallāhu ahad (A) "Say: He is Allah, the One and Only." The first line of the verse *Sūratul-Ikhlās* (Holy Qur'an: CXII).

Qur'ān (A) The Holy Qur'an is the words of God that came from His power and were revealed to Prophet Muhammad ⊕ in 6,666 *āyāt,* or verses. These revelations, or *wahys,* came from Allah to His Messenger through the Angel Gabriel ⊛.

The *Qur'ān* also exists within the heart of man. This original *Qur'ān* is a wealth that was entrusted to man by Allah in the world of the pure souls ['*ālamul-arwāh*]. The *Qur'ān* is the form of beauty, the lights and lives of grace that resonated, resplended, and descended from Allah. Those lives are forever imperishable. The *Qur'ān* is a light that is indestructible, imperishable. It is a light, a life, a power—His power. These explanations that Allah gives do not come from the outside, but from within, deep within. In all His creations He exists as life [*hayāt*] within the light which is His one hundred beautiful names of grace, His *asmā'ul-husnā*. Existing as life, He gives explanations in the form of light rays from within, from the wisdom which is His light, the *Nūr.* That is the *Qur'ān*. It is also the *guru* and the *rasūl*, the beautiful light form which explains from within.

Qutb (A) One who functions in the state of divine analytic wisdom [*pahuth arivu*], the sixth level of consciousness. The one who, having measured the length and breadth of the seven oceans of the base desires, raises up the ship of life that lies buried in the ocean of *māyā*, and rescues it from that ocean of desires. The *qutbiyyat* is the grace, the vibration, and the wisdom of Allah's essence that awakens true faith [*īmān*], restores the twelve weapons of the *Qutb* from the ocean of *māyā*, and returns the life to the form of purity it had in *arwāh*, when it emerged from Allah. *Qutb* is also a title used for the great holy men of Islam.

Qutbhū (A) Like Allah and *Allāhu*, the words *Qutb* and *Qutbhū* are very similar, except that *Qutb* merely refers to or addresses one who embodies divine analytic wisdom and *Qutbhū* calls to him with a great depth of feeling.

qutbiyyat (A) The wisdom of the *Qutb;* the sixth level of consciousness; divine analytic wisdom or *pahuth arivu;* the wisdom which explains the truth of God; the wisdom that is the power of the *Qutb*.

Rabb (A) The Lord, God; the One who creates everything; the One who awakens everything; the One who manifests all things and then protects them.

Rahmān (A) The Most Gracious, Most Merciful. *Ar-Rahmān*—one of the ninety-nine beautiful names of Allah [*asmā'ul-husnā*]. The One who rules is forever ruling with His three thousand compassionate, benevolent qualities. He has no anger at all. His duty is only to protect and sustain.

rahmat (A) God's grace; His mercy. For all creations, He alone is the wealth. He is the wealth for life [*hayāt*] and for all creations. He is the only wealth, the wealth of absolute faith [*īmān*].

rahmatul-'ālamīn (A) The mercy and compassion for all the universes; the One who gives all creations everything they ask for or desire. He is the One who made all the creations appear by saying, "*Kun!*" Allah is the Ruler of fathomless grace, the One of incomparable love. No love compares to His love. His grace has no end. That is how it is. Because of this, whenever one needs God's love, whatever his heart needs, or whatever he needs for his hunger or thirst, or for anything, his needs are satisfied through Allah's *rahmat* [mercy]. That is why He is called the *rahmatul-'ālamīn*, He provides the wondrous blessings [*mubārakāt*] for the three worlds of *awwal*, *dunyā*, and *ākhirah* [the beginning, this world, and the hereafter]. Whatever the soul needs; whatever the world needs; whatever creation needs; whatever the earth, fire, water, air, and ether need; whatever wisdom needs, He will give. He is the *rahmatul-'ālamīn* for the three worlds. He will give the treasure which is the *mubārakāt*, the wealth of the three worlds. The soul needs the purity of God, and He will give that. Wisdom needs the soul, and He will give that. This grace is within Him. He says, "I have that *rahmat*, that fathomless grace and incomparable love. Because I am the Ruler of fathomless grace, the One who is incomparable love, this is My work." He is the *rahmatul-'ālamīn*.

rak'at (A) A bowing; to surrender one's heart entirely to God and prostrate to Him. In the five times prayer of Islam, a *rak'at* is one set of a series of motions consisting of standing and bowing, followed by two prostrations.

rāsis (T) Zodiac signs.

rasūl (A) A messenger, usually referring to the Prophet Muhammad ﷺ. A *rasūl* is one who accepts God totally, not accepting anything else as God; one who accepts the words and actions of God and acts according to them; one who fulfills God's commandments. The *rasūls* followed the commandments that came down to them, each at their particular time in history.

Rasūl ﷺ (A) Allah's Messenger, Muhammad ﷺ is His essence [*dhāt*], the resplendence that emerged from His effulgence, shining radiant, as His Messenger ﷺ. Muhammad ﷺ, the manifestation of that resplendence, discourses on the explanations of luminous wisdom which he imparts to Allah's creations. He is the one who begs for truth from Allah and intercedes with prayers for all of Allah's creations and for his followers. Therefore, Allah has anointed His *Rasūl*, the Prophet Muhammad ﷺ, with the title, *The Messenger who is the savior for both worlds*.

The word *rasūl* can be used to refer to any of Allah's apostles or messengers. *See also rasūl.*

rizq (A) Nourishment; food; sustenance; that which is given as true food and provision by *ar-Razzāq*, the Provider. There is a story about when Solomon ؑ, son of David ؑ, who once offered to feed all the creations in the world, but he could not even satisfy the hunger of the first fish who showed up. That fish swallowed everything Solomon ؑ had to offer, and after that it was still howling, "I am hungry! I am thirsty!" At that point Solomon ☉ begged Allah to save him so the fish would not eat him. The fish still had its mouth open in hunger, but as soon as Allah sent down the tiniest fragment of an atom of food and of water and these two tiny dots went in, the fish closed its mouth and said, "*Al-hamdu lillāh!* All praise is to Allah alone!" That is what is called *rizq*— the atom of nourishment that comes from God. It is just one atom, and that is the *rizq* which feeds man's *īmān* [absolute faith, certitude, and determination]. All the rest of the food that comes from the world is merely straw and hay for man's desires [*nafs*]. But the *rizq* is the food that comes from Allah as nourishment. It is the beauty that comes directly from Allah. The name *Anna Muhammad* is given to this food. *Anna* is the Tamil word for food. *Muhammad* means the beautiful form. *Anna* is that *rizq*, the provision, the food which is Allah's beauty. *'Ishq* is what must be stripped away and discarded from that *rizq*. *'Ishq* is desire; that is the world.

rūh (A) Soul; the essential life [*hayāt*]. Of the six kinds of life, the *rūh* is the light life that comes as rays from the *Nūr*. It has no veils. It is not hidden from Allah, from truth. It does not die; it exists forever. Such is the *rūh*, or soul, the light-life, a life that has received the grace of Allah, the treasure for all three worlds. The other five kinds of life—earth-life, water-life, air-life, fire-life, and ether-life—all disappear and go away, but this life, the light-life, or *rūh*, never disappears. It exists forever.

rukū' (A) Bowing, during the five-times prayer of Islam while saying, "*Subhāna Rabbiyal-'azīm:* Glory be to my Lord, the great One!"

sabab (U) Meaning.

sabūr (A) Inner patience. Patience is Allah's treasure chest. Going within this treasure chest, reflecting and having forbearance is *sabūr*. Going even deeper within and contemplating is *shakūr*, and still deeper is *tawakkul*, or handing the responsibility over to Allah. Surrendering everything to God means that the person no longer exists. Once one surrenders to God, he does not exist. The good and bad do not affect him, for he is not there.

sadalam (T) Form; body. There are many meanings for *sadalam*, such as form or shadow. There is a shadow form within the body. There is also a shadow form, a *sadalam*, in dreams, or in thoughts. Everything that God has made to appear has a *sadalam*. All that has been made out of the five elements is a *sadalam*. There are many meanings for that word. It can also be translated as 'form'. All the things that have form have a shadow. Everything that is composed of the five elements (earth, fire, water, air, and ether) and that has blood circulating is also called *sadalam*.

sadaqah (A) Charity; almsgiving; contributions to the poor; the third obligatory duty in Islam, which requires Muslims to give a certain percentage of their income to the needy and poor.

saivam (T) Inner purity. In common usage it refers to the worship of the deity Shiva, the religion of Hinduism, and to vegetarianism. But in the context of this book, it is often meant to be synonymous with Islam. Nothingness is *saivam*. Like a zero, like a circle, it has no beginning or end. *Saivam* means purity, something that has no form. *Īmān-Islām* also means purity. *Īmān* is purity, something without blemish or fault. *Saivam* is something that exists forever without beginning or end, without fault, and without destruction.

In Hinduism, *saivam* refers to one who does not eat meat or fish. But bulls and goats are not *saivam*, even though they do not eat meat or fish. Some birds eat only fruits, but they cannot be called *saivam*. *Saivam* has an altogether deeper meaning.

Only *īmān* can be called Islam. Islam means the purity that does not hurt the heart of another or cause pain to anyone. This is also *saivam*. It is the state in which all the benevolent and compassionate qualities of God are complete, and one shows all lives the same love as for his own life. *Saivam* means not hurting another life, not destroying or devouring the heart of another, not backbiting, not acting deceitfully toward others. That is Islam. It is purity. That state is also called *saivam*. Truth is called *saivam*. That is *Īmān-Islām*. That plenitude, that faultless state, is known as *saivam*. It is not just a matter of whether one eats meat or not. True *saivam* is *Īmān-Islām*.

sajdah (A) To prostrate oneself in prayer. *Sajdah* is dedicating oneself to the One and handing over one's body, possessions, and soul to Him alone. Returning His kingdom, His *qalb*, and His truth to Him, surrendering these things to Him alone is *sajdah*. That is *vanakkam*, or worship.

salām (A) Peace; the peace of God. Greetings! There are many meanings to the word *salām*. When we say *salām*, it means that in God's name or in the presence of God, both of us become one without any division; both of us are in a state of unity, a state of peace. *Salām* is paying obeisance to Allah alone and returning His name of purity to Him. *See also salawāt*.

salāt (A) Blessing or prayer. Specifically, it is the prayer that is done five times daily by Muslims. It is the second obligatory duty [*fard*] in Islam.

salawāt (A) Prayers; blessings; glorification. Giving *salāms* and *salawāt* is the practice of praising, glorifying, and invoking Allah, and beseeching peace for the *Rasūl* ☾, the prophets, and the angels and other exalted beings.

About this practice Bawa Muhaiyaddeen says: When you offer a single *salām* or *salawāt*, you receive thirty *salāms* or *salawāt* in return. You receive the *salāms* of Allah, the *salāms* of the *Rasūl* ⏾, the *salāms* of the angels and heavenly beings. Every *salām*, every glorification that you offer from your mouth is returned multiplied many times through the countless mouths that Allah has created.

When you praise Muhammad ⏾, when you pay *salāms* to Muhammad ⏾, they come right back to you, almost like an echo. The praise that you offer to Allah, the *Rasūl* ⏾, and the heavenly beings comes back to you as your own treasure, your own wealth. When you offer *salāms* and *salawāt*, you will find that that praise lights up your own face and heart. You may think you are praising only Muhammad ⏾, but since Muhammad ⏾ resides within you, that praise is reflected back to benefit you, and that radiance comes forth from within your heart. This is the reason that the *salawāt* is considered to be very exalted. *See also sallallāhu 'alaihi wa sallam.*

sallallāhu 'alaihi wa sallam (A) "God bless him and grant him peace." A supplication traditionally spoken after mentioning the name of Prophet Muhammad ⏾. Denoted in the text with ⏾. Acknowledging Allah's commandments and the words brought by His Messenger, accepting them and praising them is *sallallāhu 'alaihi wa sallam*. *Salawāt* is to recite the name of Allah, praising Him and His *Rasūl* ⏾. *See also salawāt.*

saththu (T) God's essence or power. *Saththu* is different from *shaktis*. They are just energies. *Saththu* is the life or strength of God's power.

Satthiya Vētham (T) The truth of Allah and the resplendence of this truth is the *vētham* [scripture] for all creations. The *Satthiya Vētham* [true scripture] is Allah's *vētham*. It is the scripture for human beings, the clarity and justice of His commandments and His truth. Fulfilling Allah's commandments and truth in one's life and acting accordingly is *Satthiya Vētham*.

sayyid (A) A descendant of Prophet Muhammad ⏾.

shaikh (A) A spiritual guide, master, teacher, or *guru*. Everything we see teaches us something. Therefore, everything we look at is a teacher, a *shaikh*. However if one is a true *shaikh*, he must be within Allah's truth, His justice, His commandments, and His purity. A true *shaikh* will have the four virtuous qualities [*thānam, nithānam, avathānam,* and *gnānam*]. *Thānam*, or surrender, is dedicating oneself to Allah and following His commandments without any wavering. *Nithānam*, or balance, is focusing on Allah alone, standing in His gaze and walking toward Him without the slightest deviation. *Avathānam*, or concentration, is to place your careful attention upon acting with God's qualities and using great caution in walking the path of the justice of God's truth, for hell is on one side and the world on the other, mind is on one side and desire on the other. One who has followed that path in this way is in the state of the wisdom called *gnānam*. *Gnānam* is the wisdom of the *kursī*, the wisdom which is the *qutbiyyat*. One who has established that state and acts in that manner is a *shaikh*. He is the one *shaikh* for the beginningless beginning, for this world, and for the next world [*awwal, dunyā,* and *ākhirah*].

shaitān (A) Satan; *iblīs*. The one who was born from the fire of anger, jealousy, deceit, arrogance, pride, and the egoism of 'I' is satan. Anger is the fire that will destroy everything, both good and bad, without discrimination.. Satan was created from fire. He is one of the *jinns*. One who has the fire of anger is satan. Those qualities emerge from fire. Fire is anger, jealousy, arrogance, deceit, egoism of the 'I', attacking others, and hitting others. It is from these qualities, from the fire of hell, that satan emerged. On the other hand, one who has the qualities of Allah is an *insān*, a human being, a representation of Allah. Such a one has nothing other than Allah and Allah's qualities, actions, gaze, fragrance, and speech. Such a one acquires these qualities, abides by them, and thus attains Allah's beauty. Satan is all the opposite qualities, like hurting others, talking behind someone's back, being angry, being unjust, striking others, murdering others, using intoxicants, stealing, lying, having base desires and lust and all the bad qualities which lead to bad actions. These qualities and their energies are the qualities of darkness and hell. One who acquires the qualities of hell is a satan.

shakti(s) (T) The forces or energies arising from the five elements.

shakūr (A) Contentment arising out of gratitude; the state within the inner patience known as *sabūr;* that which is kept within the treasure chest of patience. *Yā Shakūr*—one of the ninety-nine beautiful names of Allah. To have *shakūr* with the help of the One who is *Yā Shakūr* is true *shakūr*.

sharī'at (A) The first step of the five steps of spiritual ascendence [*sharī'at, tarīqat, haqīqat, ma'rifat,* and *sūfiyyat*]. Since man was created out of the five elements (earth, fire, water, air, and ether), since he has within him both light and darkness, good and bad, truth and falsehood, and heaven and hell, he must know the good from the bad. Understanding what is right and what is wrong is *sharī'at*. Discarding what is bad and accepting what is good and acting accordingly is *sharī'at*. Lit. the law.

sharr (A) That which is wrong, bad, or evil, as opposed to that which is good, or *khair*. Everything that has been created is perishable and is *sharr*. Whatever is imperishable and exists forever is *khair*. We must strengthen that which is imperishable and discard that which is perishable [*sharr*]. *Sharr* is subject to change and must be discarded with the wisdom of *īmān*.

shart (A) To put into practice the conditions laid down by Allah, the conditions that must be fulfilled in prayer according to Allah's commandments.

shirk (A) A fault. Anything that is not acceptable to Allah is *shirk*, while everything that is acceptable to Allah is purity. *Shirk* is everything that has been discarded from Allah. Lit. idolatry; associating anything with God.

sifāt (A) Creation; that which is manifested. *Sifāt* is the creation, while *dhāt* is the essence. *Sifāt* is everything that has appeared from the *sukūn*, everything that arose when the word *"Kun"* was spoken. Whatever has appeared in form is *sifāt*.

sirr (A) Secret; referring to Allah's secret hidden within man, a secret which man must uncover. God is the One who knows everything. Therefore, there are no secrets hidden from God. The life of one who does not know Allah is a secret. His is a transient, unstable life.

Sivan (T) Adam ☙.

subh (A) The first of the five times prayer of Islam. Also known as *fajr*. Understanding the place where one appeared, understanding the time one appeared, and understanding one's own appearance is *subh*. To understand this and to worship Allah and prostrate before Him is *subh*. It is the understanding of how one first appeared and then praying to the only One worthy of worship. It is the time when one emerges from the darkness of *māyā* to the light and understands how he emerged. This is *subh*. Coming out of *māyā*, knowing God and worshiping Him is *subh*.

Subhānallāhi Kalimah (A) *Subhānallāhi wal-hamdu lillāhi wa lā ilāha ill-Allāhu, wallāhu akbar. Wa lā hawla wa lā quwwata illā billāhi wa huwal-'alīyul-'azīm:* Glory be to God, and all praise is to God, and none is god except Allah, and Allah is most great, and none has the majesty or the power to sustain except for God, and He is the majesty, the supreme in glory. Also known as *tasbīh*, or the Third *Kalimah*.

Sufi (A) One in the state of *sūfiyyat*, a mystic in Islam, one who has seen God within himself with the eye of certainty ['*ainul-yaqīn*].

sūfi gnānam (A & T) The wisdom of a Sufi. To speak without speaking, realize without realizing, pray without praying, and worship without worshiping is *sūfi gnānam*. To go beyond the four steps [*sharī'at, tarīqat, haqīqat,* and *ma'rifat*] to the fifth is *sūfiyyat* or *sūfi gnānam*. To attain the state of having Allah's gaze, His qualities, His actions, His breath and speech, His sound, and His *qalb* [innermost heart], and to worship Allah in that state is *sūfī gnānam*. There is no sound or speech at this time.

sūfiyyat (A) The fifth level of spiritual ascendance, the state of one who has transcended the four religions and has merged with God. *See also sūfī gnānam.*

sukūn (A) In Arabic, a graphic symbol, resembling a tiny circle (˚) which denotes a consonant with no vowel. Lit. silent; quiet.

sūpi (T) Baby's pacifier or soother. Something a baby sucks on that provides temporary comfort but no nourishment. Bawa Muhaiyaddeen frequently puns on the words *sūpi* and *sūfī*.

sūrat (A) Form, or body. The body of man is made up of the five elements: earth, fire, water, air, and ether.

Sūrat Muhammad (A) The form of Prophet Muhammad ☺.

Sūratul-Fātihah (A) The opening chapter of the Holy Qur'an; In Islam, the *Sūratul-Fātihah* is recited at the beginning of every prayer.
    The inner form of man; clarity in understanding the four elements of the body (earth, fire, water, and air), and the realization of the self and Allah within. Within man is the *Sūratul-Fātihah*, and within the *Sūratul-Fātihah* is the inner form of man. If we split open that inner form, we can see within it Allah's words, His qualities, His actions, His three thousand divine attributes, and His ninety-nine powers [*wilāyāt*]. That is the inner form of man [*sūratul-insān*].
    To see all these within, the *Sūratul-Fātihah* must be split open with wisdom. It must be opened by the ocean of divine knowledge [*bahrul-'ilm*]. Opening one's heart [*qalb*], opening one's form [*sūrat*] and looking within, at his own form—that is the *Sūratul-Fātihah*. What is recited on the outside is the *Al-hamdu Sūrat*. The outer meaning is on the first level of spiritual ascendance [*sharī'at*], whereas the inner meaning is the essence [*dhāt*]. *Fātihah* means literally to open out. It is to open the heart and look within. *See also sūratul-insān; Ummul-Qur'ān.*

Sūratul-Ikhlās (A) The Chapter of Sincerity, or Purity, the 112th chapter of the Holy Qur'an. It proclaims the unity, the absoluteness, of the Divine Essence, indicated by the word *Huwa* [He] which is the name of the Essence. It is said to have the value of one third of the entire *Qur'ān*, and, except for the opening chapter, the *Sūratul-Fātihah* is the most often repeated chapter of the *Qur'ān*.

sūratul-insān (A) The form, or body, of man. Man's physical body is formed of the five elements, but the inner subtle body is composed of the twenty-eight letters of the Arabic alphabet. The *Thiru Qur'ān*, including all 6,666 verses, is contained and compressed within these letters. Thus the subtle form of *insān* is the *Qur'ān*. The inner *Qur'ān*, formed of these letters of light, is the *sūratul-insān*. *Sūratul-insān* has within it the light of Allah, the resplendent form of the *Qur'ān*. *Sūratul-insān* is the inner *Qur'ān*. *Sūratul-Fātihah* is Allah's *Qur'ān*. You need to see this *Qur'ān*. If you see His *Qur'ān* and recite it, you will perceive only Allah's commandments there. Understanding this is *Sūratul-Fātihah*. It is to know yourself. When you know yourself you will know your *Rabb*, your Lord, and when you know your *Rabb*, you will know His creations. When you know the creations of the *Rabb*, you can be an emperor to those creations. You can become a *sayyid* or a *shaikh*. You can correct them, show them the good path, and take them on that path.

sūriya kalai (T) The breath of divine analytic wisdom, the indrawn breath, the breath of the *qutbiyyat* or light. *Chandira kalai*, in contrast, is the breath of the world, the breath of the seven colors: earth, fire, water, air, ether, mind, and desire.

tarīqat (A) The second of the five steps of spiritual ascendance; unswerving and complete acceptance of the good and the carrying out of every action accordingly; the truth of intention, certitude, determination, faith, patience, and duty. Lit. the path.

tasbīh (A) The glorification of God as the Supreme Being, expressed by the word 'Subhānallāh', and also by the Third *Kalimah*. *Tasbīh* is to purify the heart, the shrine in which the Pure One resides.

tawakkul-'alallāh (A) Absolute trust and surrender; handing over to God the entire responsibility for everything; to take each thing to Allah and hand over the entire responsibility to Him. This is a state of total surrender. After that the 'I' does not exist. Whatever happens as a result—whether it be good or bad—is no longer one's responsibility. It has been given over to God. Lit. trust in Allah. *See also sabūr.*

Thiruchudar (T) The Triple Flame. Bawa Muhaiyaddeen ☺ explains that these three Arabic letters—*alif*, *lām*, and *mīm*—represent the Triple Flame, the Triple Effulgence, the true form of man. *Alif* (ا) is Allah, the Creator. *Lām* (ل) is the *Nūr*, the light of wisdom. And *mīm* (م) is Muhammad ☺ (the created manifestation, the light of the soul). Who are you? You are Muhammad ☺. What is inside you? The light, the *lām*. That is wisdom. What is within that? God, the *alif*, who is without sound. All three are joined together in one form, the body; within the body is the light, and within the light is the mystery. This is the explanation of the relationship between the *Rabb*, the Creator, and *insān*, the created being.

Thiru-Guru-Ān (T) *Thiru* means triple or three, *guru* means a spiritual teacher or *shaikh*, *ān* means a male. Bawa Muhaiyaddeen explains that Allah is the only male, defining a male as one who has no illusion within him. Thus, all creations are female in search of the one male.

Thiru Marai or *Thiru Qur'ān* (T & A) The original *Qur'ān*; the inner *Qur'ān* inscribed within the heart. All the secrets and the essence of the three worlds of *awwal*, *dunyā*, and *ākhirah* [the beginning of creation, the physical world, and the hereafter] have been buried and concealed by Allah within the *Thiru Qur'ān*. Within it, He has concealed the explanations of the essence of grace [*dhāt*] and of the manifestations of creation [*sifāt*]. There He has concealed the *alif*, *lām*, and *mīm*; these three are the essence. That is why it is called the *Thiru Qur'ān*. *Thiru* means triple in Tamil.

Literally, *marai* means holy scriptures, and as such it refers to the scriptures and words of every religion. In this sense it is used to describe the book called the Holy Qur'an. But as Bawa Muhaiyaddeen explains, it is the manifestation of the conscience of God in every age to every nation, revealing to mankind the means of attaining Him. This is the inner *Qur'ān*, the original *Qur'ān*, which becomes manifest from time to time, revealing the guidelines of human conduct in relation to spiritual evolution. If God is the reality immanent within man, then the voice of God (the revelation that proceeds from the *Nūr*, the *perr arivu*) is called *Thiru Marai*.

Thiru Qur'ān (T & A) *See Thiru Marai.*

tholuhai (T) Prayer; the performance of a prayer in which one remembers only God to the exclusion of everything else. Also refers to the five times prayer of Islam.

Ūmaiyan (T) One who is silent; one who does not speak, a term that refers to God.

ummī (A) Silent; unlettered. An *ummī* is one who keeps only Allah, Allah's grace, His truth, His gaze, and His qualities, and discards everything else in the world, the selfishness and all the sights and sounds. An *ummī* keeps nothing but Allah's wisdom within him; he keeps nothing but the speech and words of Allah, nothing but the actions of Allah, and nothing but the gaze of Allah with him. He keeps within him only that which belongs to Allah and discards everything else that comes along. Lit. one who is illiterate.

Ummul-Qur'ān (A) The 'source' or 'mother' of the *Qur'ān*; the eternal source of all the revelations to all the prophets. It is also known as the *Ummul-Kitāb*. It is a divine, indestructible tablet on which all is recorded. It is the silent *Qur'ān* which exists as a mystery within the heart [*qalb*] of each person. The name *Ummul-Qur'ān* is also used to refer to the *Sūratul-Fātihah*, or the opening chapter of the *Qur'ān*. It is said that within the 124 letters of the *Sūratul-Fātihah* is contained the meaning of the entire *Qur'ān*. Lit. the mother, or source of the book.

unarchi (T) Awareness, the second of the seven levels of wisdom innate in man. *See also* Appendix: The Seven Levels of Consciousness.

unarvu (T) Feeling or perception, the first of the seven levels of wisdom innate in man. *See also* Appendix: The Seven Levels of Consciousness.

Unnai thavira veru oru āndavan illai (T) There is no God other than You. There is none other who rules all three worlds.

vanakkam (T) Worship. Other than Allah there is none worthy of worship. *Vanakkam* is to know Him completely, and, without any feeling of 'I', to transform the *sūrat* [form] and qualities of man and to acquire the *sūrat* and qualities of Allah, and, standing as Him, to worship Him. Thus, Allah worships Allah. When the form and qualities of man change into the qualities and *sūrat* of Allah and God worships God, that is *vanakkam*.

vīna (T) A stringed musical instrument. A lute from India, usually with seven strings and two octaves.

wahy (A) Revelation; inspiration from God; the inspired word of God revealed to a prophet; the commandments or words of God transmitted by the Archangel Gabriel ☙. Revelations have come to Adam ☙, Moses ☙, and various other prophets, but Prophet Muhammad ☙ received 6,666 revelations. The histories of all the earlier prophets were included within the revelations given to Prophet Muhammad ☙.
   Wahys are the commandments given by Allah. They are the benevolences bestowed by Allah. They are His *rahmat*, or wealth of grace, the grace of divine knowledge, the grace of truth, the grace of *īmān*, the grace of wisdom, and the grace of perfect purity.

waqt (A) Time of prayer. In the religion of Islam, there are five specified *waqts*, or times of prayer, each day. But truly, there is only one *waqt*; that is the prayer that never ends, wherein one is in direct communication with God and has merged with Him.

wilāyāt (A) God's power which has been revealed and manifested through His actions; the miraculous names and actions of God; the powers of His attributes through which all creations came into existence.

The worldly meaning for *wilāyāt* is miracles and forces that are acquired by chanting praises to one or more of the five elements (earth, fire, water, air, and ether), to *jinns*, demons and ghosts. *Mantras* are chanted to summon these elements in order to control them and use them to perform supernatural feats. The miracles performed in this way are known in Tamil as *sitthis* and in Arabic as *wilāyāt*. They are not related to the power of Allah.

When one dedicates himself to Allah, he has no miracles, praise, or anything else in this world. In that state, only Allah worships Allah, only Allah shows the way to Allah. Such a man praises nothing other than Allah and has no miracles to perform.

In the state of *qutbiyyat*, Allah's devotees receive grace from the compassionate gaze of Allah. As soon as one intends Allah, His gaze falls on them. That which is given through His divine grace is Allah's power, His *wilāyāt*. As soon as one thinks about something, Allah makes it happen. God makes things happen as soon as His devotees intend it. As soon as God glances at them, things happen. It is not done by the devotees, it is done by Allah, by Allah's power, His *wilāyāt*.

Yā (A) The vocative 'O!'. An invocation of praise and glory.

Yā Rabbal-'ālamīn (A) O Lord of all the universes.

Yaman (T) The Tamil word for 'Izrā'īl ☽, the Angel of Death.

yuga (T) A period of fifty million years in the world's existence. Each cycle of creation consists of four *yugas*, or two hundred million years. This universe is now nearing the end of the fourth *yuga*.

Zabūr, Jabrat, Injīl, and *Furqān* (A) The four scriptures, or the four steps of spiritual ascendance. The inner form of man [*sūratul-insān*] is made up of the four religions. The four religions constitute his body.

First is *Zabūr* [Hinduism], the scripture relating to the creation of form, the appearance of man. In the body, Hinduism relates to the area below the waist.

Second is *Jabrat*, Fire Worship. This relates to hunger, disease, and old age. This is the area of the stomach.

Third is *Injīl*, Christianity. This is the region of the heart which is filled with thoughts, emotions, spirits, vapors, many tens of millions of forms, the five elements, mind and desire, and four hundred trillion, ten thousand types of spiritual worship.

Fourth is *Furqān*, the scriptures sent down to Moses ☽ and Muhammad ﷺ. This corresponds to the head. It is made up of the seven causes (two eyes, two ears, two nostrils, and one mouth), and through these it gives explanations.

To study and understand these four religions as four steps and to understand the difference between good and evil is the function of the head, or *Furqān*. The head is the leader or chief for all four religions. If there is no head, the form cannot be identified, for there are no identifying marks. It is the head that sees, using the seven faculties, which are the identifying signs. To see with the eyes, to hear with the ears, to smell through the nostrils, to speak or taste with the mouth, to give information and to explain through wisdom, to transmit explanations to the *qalb*, or heart, to realize and understand the diffe.ence between good and evil, to take up whatever is good, to show it, and to transmit the meaning to the heart—that is *Furqān*. The head of every man is called *Furqān*.

zakāt (A) Charity; one of the five obligatory duties of Islam—to give a portion of one's income to the poor.

zamzam (A) A never-ending wellspring near the place where the *Ka'bah* stands today, which gushed forth originally for Ishmael ⊛ and his mother, Hagar ⊛. It is said to flow from the spring of *kauthar* [abundance] in paradise.

    Zamzam is the honey that oozes from the certitude of faith [*īmān*] in the heart of wisdom. There are two *zamzam* wells in the body. From one, water oozes into the throat from the well which is the body. This water smells like ordinary water. But through the other *zamzam* well, fragrant honey oozes from the *īmān* of Allah's divine knowledge.

zīnat (A) The beauty of God which enamors all creations. If one becomes a true man, he will acquire the beauty of God.

zuhr (A) The noontime prayer; the second of the five times prayer of Islam. This is the period of torpor when one is intoxicated by the seven base desires. The essences of the seven forces (earth, fire, water, air, ether, mind, and desire) function in this period. Noon, or midday, represents adolescence, the period of man's life when mind, desire, and illusion surround him. Hell is on one side, mind and desire are on the other side. Wisdom and truth exist in the center. This is the period in which you have to decide which way you wish to go. Hell is on one side, illusion is on the other, and the *Rabb* or Lord, the path of justice on which you must travel, is in the center.

    You need to understand all these paths and decide which to walk on. Having decided, you must walk carefully. If you fall to one side *māyā* will grab you, and if you fall to the other side hell will grab you. You have to determine how to achieve a balance and then take the correct path. It is in this period of your life that you have to understand and choose your path. This is *zuhr*.

Books by M. R. Bawa Muhaiyaddeen

Truth & Light: brief explanations

Songs of God's Grace

The Divine Luminous Wisdom That Dispels the Darkness

Wisdom of the Divine (Vols. 1–5)

The Guidebook to the True Secret of the Heart (Vols. 1, 2)

God, His Prophets and His Children

Four Steps to Pure Iman

The Wisdom of Man

A Book of God's Love

My Love You My Children:
101 Stories for Children of All Ages

Come to the Secret Garden: Sufi Tales of Wisdom

The Golden Words of a Sufi Sheikh

The Tasty, Economical Cookbook (Vols. 1, 2)

Sheikh and Disciple

Maya Veeram or The Forces of Illusion

Asma'ul-Husna: The 99 Beautiful Names of Allah

Islam and World Peace: Explanations of a Sufi

A Mystical Journey

Questions of Life—Answers of Wisdom

Treasures of the Heart: Sufi Stories for Young Children

To Die Before Death: The Sufi Way of Life

A Song of Muhammad ﷺ

Hajj: The Inner Pilgrimage

Gems of Wisdom series—
Vol. 1: The Value of Good Qualities
Vol. 2: Beyond Mind and Desire
Vol. 3: The Innermost Heart
Vol. 4: Come to Prayer

A Contemporary Sufi Speaks—
To Teenagers and Parents
On the Signs of Destruction
On Peace of Mind
On the True Meaning of Sufism
On Unity: The Legacy of the Prophets
The Meaning of Fellowship
Mind, Desire, and the Billboards of the World

Foreign Language Publications—
Ein Zeitgenössischer Sufi Spricht über Inneren Frieden
(A Contemporary Sufi Speaks on Peace of Mind—
German Translation)

Deux Discours tirés du Livre L'Islam et la Paix Mondiale:
Explications d'un Soufi
(Two Discourses from the Book Islam and World Peace:
Explanations of a Sufi—French Translation)

For free catalog or book information call:
(888) 786-1786

About the
Bawa Muhaiyaddeen Fellowship

Muhammad Raheem Bawa Muhaiyaddeen ☺, a Sufi mystic from Sri Lanka, was a man of extraordinary wisdom and compassion. For over seventy years he shared his knowledge and experience with people of every race and religion and from all walks of life.

The central branch of The Bawa Muhaiyaddeen Fellowship is located in Philadelphia, Pennsylvania. It was Bawa Muhaiyaddeen's residence while he was in the United States until his death in December 1986. The Fellowship continues to serve as a meeting house and a reservoir of people and materials for all who are interested in his teachings.

Also located on the same property is The Mosque of Shaikh Muhammad Raheem Bawa Muhaiyaddeen where the daily five times of prayer and Friday congregational prayers are held. An hour west of the Fellowship is the *Mazār*, or tomb, of M. R. Bawa Muhaiyaddeen which is open for visitation.

For further information write or phone:

The Bawa Muhaiyaddeen Fellowship
5820 Overbrook Avenue
Philadelphia, Pennsylvania 19131

(215) 879-8604
(24 hour answering machine)

E-mail Address: info@bmf.org
Web Address: http://www.bmf.org

If you would like to visit the Fellowship or obtain a schedule of current events or branch locations and meetings, please write, phone, or E-mail *Attn: Visitor Information.*

Made in the USA
San Bernardino, CA
04 August 2020